Two on a Boat

How to Keep it Afloat

A LIGHT-HEARTED LOOK AT HOW UNDERSTANDING GENDER DIFFERENCES CAN HELP COUPLES CREATE HARMONY ON THE SEAS OF LIFE AND ON A BOAT.

BY JOSIPHINE "CAPTAIN JOSIE" LONGO

To My Students - My Friends

This book is dedicated to all my students who became my friends in the short time we spent together.

To those, who suggested the books for me to read on gender differences . To those who encouraged me, to write this book. Those who believed in my methods and suggestions for a better way to sail together.

This is also for every one of my friends who encouraged me to pursue this book and to all my students who inspired and educated me. Even the problem children.

To all the couples that have stayed married through thick and thin, you truly encourage and inspire me. And finally, to all those students who gave me the stories from our own little adventures aboard the Tididi. See you on the sea...

Also a huge thanks to my mother, Emma and sister, Marian, without their help in proofing the book as well as Tanya Hackney (and family), my editing mentor, who took this book to the next level, one of my sailing students who has become a very special sailing and spiritual friend.

CONTENTS

TWO ON A BOAT How to Keep it Afloat

INTRODUCTION

You will immediately find that this is not one of those books that starts out with the author boasting of her great success and accomplishments on the high seas. My claim to fame is that I was, in fact, just the opposite when it came to relationships at sea. I am willing to reveal my experiences and lack of success in the hopes that I can help and encourage others to achieve their goals and follow their dreams.

Among my earliest memories are times on a small powerboat in Connecticut in search of lobster, with my dad at the helm. I remember sitting on the bow in a bulky life jacket at four or five years old and loving it. Thirty years later, I sat at the helm of a sailboat with a boyfriend yelling "Head up, head up!" I yelled back to him, "My head is up, but which way do you want me to turn?" After repeatedly feeling defeated and frustrated, I knew I would have to either take sailing lessons from someone else or quit sailing. Maybe it was the boyfriend I needed to quit. In the end, I did take sailing lessons, and no longer sailed with him!

Since then, I have accomplished most of my dreams. I have single-handed my boat, lived aboard for seven years, cruised extensively, and crossed two oceans in the company of other sailors. I got my USCG captain's license, and have had the joy of teaching others to sail in formal and informal settings. After failing in the relationship department at sea, I set my sights on determining why some couples not only survive together at sea, but thrive in cramped quarters and stressful situations, while others are in constant discord.

Because of my experiences over the years, both as a woman just learning to sail and now as an accomplished sailor and instructor, I decided to write this book to help couples learn to sail, to work together like clockwork, and to approach each other with respect and understanding. I have been in both the masculine and feminine roles aboard boats and can relate to the needs of both genders. I know what it is to be reduced to tears from being misunderstood or put down, but also to have all the pressure on my shoulders to keep my boat safe and protect the lives on my vessel without displaying fear or uncertainty. And through gender research and personal experience with hundreds of couples, I have a unique approach to teaching men and women.

CB

Who should read this book? In short, everyone can benefit! Women who have been yelled at one time too many, followed orders for a long time without understanding what they were doing, or who lack confidence will find clarity and will stop feeling like there is something wrong with them when they can't understand the instruction given by husbands, boyfriends, male instructors, or sailing books written by men who simply don't understand that women process information differently. Men who sail with women and feel frustrated because they can't seem to get her to understand, or who would like a wife or partner to enjoy sailing more will find that learning where she's coming from and how to communicate better makes all the difference in the world, on a boat or on land! Couples who read the book will learn the same information and discover how to apply it together. They will improve not only their seamanship, but their relationship as well. Sailing instructors who want to meet the needs of their male and female students alike can learn how to address both gender approaches to learning and have better results with students. The principles in the book apply to both sail and power boaters, to men and women, to couples, groups and friends. It is important that everyone, from the professional to the "old salt" to the novice sailor understand gender dynamics if the dream to sail is to stay alive. Lastly, even non-boaters can benefit from my experience and advice—if a couple can learn to get along on a boat, they can get along anywhere!

℈

While instructing couples afloat and dealing with my own male shipmates, I more often found myself addressing Mars and Venus issues than seamanship issues. Men and women learn differently. While that may not be news to you, the sailing industry has been slow to catch on. Sometimes sailing schools are interested more in profit than in their students' proficiency. Others are insensitive to the needs of female students, directing teaching in a way that makes sense to men but may "lose" the women in their classes. Some couples search for a reputable school only to find the instructor is using outdated methods, or is more focused on helping them pass a test than develop confidence and teamwork. It is to correct this deficiency that I have written this book.

I've often seen the "Captain Bligh vs. Submissive Female" syndrome which can be a real pain in the stern, not to mention counterproductive to harmony onboard. I've also seen the adventurous man who inadvertently terrifies the woman in his life and can't understand her apprehensiveness onboard. And then there are those who, because they don't understand that male and female brains work differently, think there is something mentally wrong with the other person. These fallacies can alienate women to the point of abandoning ship. If they do return, it is often in a state of fear and trepidation. Sailing started out as a man's domain, but it is my desire to demonstrate that women are just as capable in all aspects of sailing, particularly when nurtured and coached in their own learning style. Those who care enough to see that women's needs are met will make a positive impact on the sailing community as a whole.

I have also watched couples mesh into effective teammates during a week-long sailing class, which enhances their desire to sail as well as their desire for each other! As each discovers the other's strengths as a sailor, they learn things about each other as a man or woman which then helps them to work together without struggle or gender battles.

This book will give you the benefit of my research on gender differences and my experience with teaching couples how men and women learn differently, how to work as a team, and how to avoid typical gender conflict.

ଔ

This book represents the culmination of all my mistakes, sailing skills, research, teaching experience, seminars and lectures. Because most of the sailing books available on the market are designed by men and for the male linear learning style, you will not find another book that approaches this subject quite like I do, and from my perspective as a woman and a teacher. I will be offering some new ideas for learning to sail in harmony, supported by humorous anecdotes, some of which you may already relate to. For those who have never mastered the basics of sailing, I offer a sneak peek at the Sailing Wind Wheel—you will never be confused again!

My goal is to look at how gender differences can affect two or more people on a boat. Learning what conflicts may arise and what is a typical male or female response and how you can do things differently will vastly improve quality of life aboard. I will explore why one partner in a relationship has such difficulty learning from the other. I will suggest different approaches for men and women and help both partners improve onboard communication.

To the guy reading this who cares about what is important to the woman in his life, I applaud you. To the lady willing to learn how to sail in order to share a new experience with the man in your life, I applaud you. When we realize that not everyone thinks like we do and take the time to learn about another's needs and wants, we can make some adaptations that work for the greater good and happiness of both. You must care about each other, or you wouldn't be together in the first place, right? So, let's use some TLC and look at meeting another's needs as well as our own. It takes both of you for this to work, so let's get down to business.

CB

Author's Note: Throughout the book, I use the words "wife, spouse, husband, partner, mate," etc. interchangeably. Sometimes I may address "you" and it may not seem to fit. Please insert the word that suits you best and ignore the rest. Just because it says "he" does not always mean it is his fault. I generalize for the purpose of illustration or giving an example of a typical scenario. It may not fit your situation perfectly, but you should still be able to get ideas for growth and improvement. I give examples and advice, but the rest is up to you!

Two on a Boat How to Keep it Afloat

ONE

SAILORS IN MY LIFE

How many times did the conversation go something like, "Well, maybe if you explain it to me so that I can understand it, I will get it" ? I would then tell him, "I may be blonde, but I'm not stupid."

I've been in every conceivable dysfunctional situation with men on boats. I've been intimidated, yelled at, made to feel stupid, argued with, talked down to, ordered around, ignored and criticized. So no matter what the situation you may find yourself in, I can probably relate. Before I dig into why things went wrong and how they could have been made better, here are a few of the stories about the sailors in my life.

ON BOATS WITH MY DAD

My father, a city boy who grew up in the Bronx, started sailing on ships at the ripe old age of fifteen. As the breadwinner for his mother and two younger brothers, he ran away from home and joined the Army. When they found out how old he was they kicked him out. So he signed up on a merchant marine ship as an able bodied seaman instead.

He spent the majority of his life on ships and in the military. He finished his military career with thirty-four years active duty, having served in the Army, Marines, Navy and the Coast Guard. He retired from the Coast Guard as a Chief Quartermaster (navigator) and has sailed the seven seas, the two poles, and received many commendations for his search and rescue efforts. He saved lives and loved the sea. This, I'm sure, is partly why I learned to love the sea.

We always lived around the water and I was always on the Coast Guard ships. However, Dad himself was very against women on the water, feeling that they were a hindrance. Hearing stories about the guys getting in trouble because of the women on board, I really don't blame him.

When it came to teaching us, his expectations were too high—he seemed to forget we were only children. Worse still, the girls could never get it right by his standards. I can still hear his voice in my head, "What is the matter with you? How many times do I have to tell you the same thing?" or "What are you, stupid? I've told you that a hundred times before!" and "Can't you do anything right?"

If you are someone (male or female) who is nodding your head right now, then I apologize for stirring up old memories. When you have been told that there is something wrong with you over and over, after a while you begin to believe it. I have experienced many of the same insecurities that hold so many women back from feeling confident on the water. In my case, these fears kept me from even experiencing this great sport until I was in my thirties.

The primary problem that keeps women from learning something new like sailing, is that they do not want to be yelled at or criticized. Does this come as a surprise? Yet there are still people out there who do not understand why women don't want to learn from them. Being insulted, belittled, or told that one has a learning problem, does not encourage or motivate anybody to continue learning a new subject, especially something like sailing.

My earliest memories include being reminded that I was stupid. It was understood that if you asked a question, you were dumb, so I didn't ask. Of course, I didn't learn anything except to stay off the boat so that I wouldn't get yelled at.

I was ten years old when my father, thinking he was being funny, decided to dunk me while I was floating in an inner tube. At the same time that he pushed my head down, his friend grabbed my ankles and jerked me under the water. I was taken by surprise and I was terrified by the experience. I felt I was being intentionally drowned! I remember the water getting up my nose and burning. This memory left a scar for life. There was nothing funny about it.

After that I didn't like swimming, surprise, surprise! As a teenager, if I told people that I was afraid of the water, they would either try to dunk me or push me in the water. I finally just stayed away from the water and learned not to trust anyone.

The idea of sailing was completely unappealing to me on every level after all of this. I didn't want to be yelled at and I was afraid of the water... why would I ever go out on a boat? However, never say "never" because life changes, people change, and the right experience can change everything.

I can also tell you that my relationship with my father changed, too. While we didn't always see eye to eye, I respected him and all of his accomplishments. We shared a bond because of our love for the sea. We had a great relationship, especially in the last years of his life. I encouraged him to write the stories of his life which he documented in his book, Sea Episodes of a Sailor by Richard Longo.

❧

SAILING WITH JACK IN THE PACIFIC NORTHWEST

It wasn't until my son was graduating high school and I was going through a divorce that I, by chance, met this sailboat racer who changed the whole course of my life. I didn't know it at the time, but it was actually a set-up from the start. My girlfriend and I were invited to go out on a boat by this guy we met at work. It was on a Friday night in July on Lake Washington, and it sounded like fun.

Being the girls that we were, I asked her, "What kind of boat?" She said, "I don't know." Then I asked, "Well how big of a boat is it?" Again she replied, "I don't know." So being a female I asked, "Well ,what should we wear?" I was clueless to say the least.

Two on a Boat How to Keep it Afloat

As I was walking down the dock, in my little denim mini-skirt, getting invitations to go sailing by all the guys on the sailboats, I thought, "Hmm, this is interesting. When I'm ready to start dating, I think I may have to come back here."

Now after several invitations to boats, a guy in dark sunglasses came up to me and said, "Are you looking for a particular boat?" With reservations, I replied with a simple "Yes." He prodded me for the name of the boat, which I told him was Kentucky Woman. He said, "Oh that's the boat I'm on, but it's not here yet."

By the time the boat arrived, this same guy was now insistent upon finding me a pair of shorts to wear. I kept repeating that I was okay, but he was adamant about wearing shorts. Well, he finally found the shorts for me and while I was below putting them on he yelled down, "You'll want to lose the panty hose too." I was getting nervous about this guy watching me so closely!

Nobody on the boat bothered to tell us what the word "tacking" meant. However, we learned quickly with that first tack. The first thing we learned was that they were not letting us go through the cockpit to get to the other side. Over the cabin top, on our knees we went, tack after tack. That night after a lot of tacking, I was forever grateful to Jack for the shorts.

Later on, Jack and I dated for a couple of years and when people would ask how we met he would always jump in and tell them, "I got her skirt off her in fifteen minutes flat." Of course, I made him tell the whole story!

I found myself suddenly immersed in this world of sailboats. Jack invited me to do more sailing and for some reason I trusted him, perhaps because he seemed to know what he was doing from the racing that first night. I thought, "He must be a decent guy if people will give him the keys to a forty-foot boat, right?"

The thing that sold me was that he made it fun and romantic. I felt safe, I didn't have to go into the water, and I was being spoiled with attention. We sailed to these wonderful remote and romantic places. I loved being in the mountains and nature so that part was easy. Besides, he did most of the work on the boat while I just had to "look pretty." (Not really, but it's always the joke of those who work to call non-participating females "boat fluff." Who cares what you're called if you are having fun, right?)

We took our first weekend sail to Port Townsend, Washington, on a forty foot C & C. He knew the right music, had the right wine and loved to cook. Wow! I was being wooed. The weather was beautiful and the scenery sailing up Puget Sound was spectacular. It was breath-taking to me to experience it from the water. I was hooked.

The first summer we dated, I flew from Lake Union on a float plane to Canada. Jack and I sailed from Campbell River on Vancouver Island back to Seattle via the San Juan Islands. Every night we were in a new place and every day was a new adventure. Being spoiled made it really easy to settle into this lifestyle. I loved the peacefulness while we were sailing and the tranquility of being in nature. I had always enjoyed hiking and camping, but seeing the mountains from the water was a new perspective. There is something about being on the water in this part of the world that soothes the soul.

We completed our trip at Rosario resort on Orcas Island. The one experience I won't forget was his determination to raise the Spinnaker and sail into the anchorage. I was terrified because it meant that I had to handle the boat at the helm, and I wasn't sure I could do it. *What if* I did something wrong? *What if* I hit another boat? *What if* something worse happened? I knew how uncertain I was at the helm. Why did he feel the need to do this now? I couldn't understand why he had do this crazy and seemingly dangerous thing.

It took us three tries, but on the third try he was successful and we came around the corner in front of the resort looking pretty cool. Before I knew it he had the anchor down and we were safe again. I didn't know if I should laugh or cry over the experience. When I think back on it, it was truly magic, but at the time I was just sure something terrible was going to happen. And it was because I really had no clue about what I was doing at the helm or what we were actually trying to do. And most importantly, why we would do such a stupid thing? To a guy, it's just a challenge, and when he succeeds, he has the sense that he has conquered and triumphed.

But what started out as magic and romance slowly changed into irritation and anxiety. I remember Jack getting aggravated with me one day when the winds were light. I could not keep the boat sailing where he wanted it and the sails kept luffing. He would yell, "Head up!" I had no idea what that meant, so he would point in the direction he wanted me to go. He would tell me to watch the arrow at the top of the mast. My neck always hurt when we went sailing because I was always looking up. "Head up!" Those were the words that I dreaded to hear.

We sailed on a variety of boats. Some were with tillers and others were with wheels. Because you steer them differently, every time I was put on the helm I would inevitably turn the wrong way. I didn't think I would ever understand what those words, "head up" meant. I would just look to the top of the mast at that arrow and try to understand what he was asking me to do. He had promised never to yell at me, so he would just give me that look of disgust instead. That look told me just how annoyed he was with me. It would take all my will power not to break down and cry.

My anxiety grew into fear the more I sailed with Jack. Once we went to Grandville Island, BC, Canada on the same boat we met on, Kentucky Woman. It was a forty foot IOR race boat with running back stays, a tiller and an open transom. I was always fearful on this boat because he had told me, "You see those things? (Referring to the running back stays.) If we don't remember to put them on, the mast could fall down." I didn't even know what they were or how to use them and now we could have something really bad happen to us. I worried all the time and just prayed he would do the right thing.

We had my son, my nephew and his friend aboard and the winds were strong off of Vancouver, BC. Jack went forward, like he always did, tweaking something or other. I had no idea what he was doing. As the wind increased and the boat started heeling more and more, I began to get nervous. I already hated being at the helm and with the strong winds, the boat was heeling more than I liked. Feeling as if we were going to tip all the way over, I responded by pulling on the tiller. (Yes, you who have tillers know I did the wrong thing.) The boat tipped even more. So what did I do? I pulled even more and made it worse. I was now frozen. It didn't seem logical to push the tiller toward the water but pulling it didn't work either. I sat there quietly paralyzed with fear, praying that he would fix it before we died.

Finally, he looked back at me and asked me if I was okay. I was about ready to break down, and all I managed to get out with my lower lip quivering was one word, "N-o-o-o-o!" He came back and took the helm and got the boat back under control. Now At that moment I would rather have been anywhere else in the world than on that boat. I don't know why I couldn't just call him and ask him to help me. I guess I didn't want to feel stupid or to have him annoyed with me again. But I also didn't want to go into the freezing cold water. I told myself, "If I get out of this alive, I'm outta' here! I am not going to do this again. I'm done with sailing and boats."

I don't know about anyone else, but I can tell you that I personally don't want to be in a place where I'm afraid, especially when it comes to falling into water that is fifty-six degrees or colder all year-round. After that experience I was increasingly reluctant to take the helm. I just didn't understand what was going on and I was always doing the wrong thing, so I would rather not steer at all.

The next trip we took was to San Diego. Jack was always good at finding us a boat. He got a thirty foot Catalina, the catch being that it had no engine. No problem—for him, that is! So off we went. We had the mainsail and a one hundred fifty percent Genoa up and it was blowing like crazy. The boat was heeled over hard with the rail in the water, which, of course, made me extremely uncomfortable. What was worse, he wanted me to go up and skirt the jib, or pull the sail off of the bow pulpit, where it was stuck.

Well, all I could do was visualize myself slipping off the boat into the icy cold water. I told him I didn't want to go up there. He told me to take the helm so he could go, but of course it had a tiller and I was even more fearful of driving the boat, so I told him I didn't want to do that either. Then he got irritated and said, "Well you need to do one or the other." Finally I agreed to go forward, after he explained how to go up on the high side. I managed to do the job without falling off the boat, but hated every second. The only good thin I can say is that his skills in handling the boat and sailing us back into the slip without an engine were impressive. But I had almost had enough.

In two years of sailing with Jack, the only explanation I got on the wind was, "You want to be down wind of a bear." Yes, you heard me right. I scratched my head, too. I understand that you want to be down wind of a bear so he doesn't smell you, but what does that have to do with sailing? Why was it so difficult for him to simply explain it to me? He never explained anything to me and I believe it was because he just didn't know how. I always just did what I was told because I would never completely understand everything that was going on. Consequently, I never improved. He would just put me on a point of sail and tell me to watch the arrow at the top of the mast. How many times did the conversation go something like, "Well, maybe if you explain it to me so that I can understand it, I will get it" ? I would then tell him, "I may be blonde, but I'm not stupid."

You would think that after sailing with this guy for two years, I learned a thing or two about sailing, right? I did learn that I was absolutely sold on the idea of sailing. I loved the physical and mental challenges, I loved the places I could go that were remote and wonderful, and I loved that I could live on a boat, go traveling and take my house with me. What I didn't like was feeling stupid and incapable.

After a trip to Desolation Sound, where we spent three weeks island hopping. I vowed that I would buy a boat and live aboard, but not with Jack. I didn't want to end up dependant on a boat partner, like so many of my female sailing friends. Looking back, I realize that everything I am doing now is a result of buying into the dream with this guy..

After deciding that the relationship wasn't going to work and that I would probably never learn anything from him, I started taking sailing classes. For three years, I sailed every weekend on boats with other people that I met through a couple of different sailing clubs. And after taking two sessions of sailing classes, I was taking boats out as the skipper, with at least one person on the boat who mostly knew what they were doing so they could help me dock the boat. Taking the sailing classes helped me to realize that I had learned a lot during my time with

Jack, but the classes filled in the missing information. I gained more confidence because I could understand what I was doing on a boat.

Five years to the week after I declared that I would buy my own boat, I did just that. I named her Tididi, which is 'I-did-it' spelled backwards. It just summed up the story of my life It had always been Jack's goal to buy a boat, to live-aboard and to sail to Tahiti, but it was I who bought the boat, lived aboard for seven years, single-handed it throughout the Bahamas and sailed as crew on a seventy foot aluminum boat, Maya, from Seattle to Tahiti. I reminded Jack that I am the woman who has fulfilled all of his dreams.

ॐ

SAILING WITH DIDIER ON TIDIDI

The trip to the Bahamas did not start out as a single-handing experience, but ended that way by my choice. I must say that it turned out to be one of the best things I ever did for myself in terms of gaining my confidence as a sailor. I learned that I could do anything and that I was self-sufficient.

I met Didier (pronounced D-D-A), at an after-race party with the Gulfstream Sail Club in Fort Lauderdale, Florida. I had just moved my boat down from Stuart, Florida back to Fort Lauderdale and the club asked me to be the committee boat. Joe, a friend in the sail club, had spent the weekend teaching me how to dock and anchor single-handed, so I was feeling pretty good about my accomplishments.

I set my goal to single-hand so that I wouldn't be dependent on anyone if I wanted to go sailing, and also because doing long passages with another person requires that one person sleep while the other person handles the boat alone. I just wanted to be confident as a mate, not set any records for single-handing my boat.

Didier was a tall, dark and handsome French guy with long black hair and an accent which could melt you instantly. He was a very good sailor with a lot of sailing experience. He had already been to all the places I wanted to go. He had lived on the Island of Moorea, in Tahiti for three years and had built his own boat. He was an engineer, an architect and carpenter. He could do anything on a boat and loved to sail. What more could a girl ask for?

He initially came to my boat to help me whip some lines but I'm sure it was a ploy to do more. The romance and dreams began. We both loved to sail and I had the boat. I was on sabbatical with a knee injury and while he nursed me back to health after surgery, we started making plans to go cruising.

My first comment to him was, "How do you feel about a woman being the captain, because I own the boat?" He said he was okay with it. This was important to me since I'd had several bad experiences with men trying to take control on my boat. I was determined not to let it happen again. We sailed together twice to the Bahamas and down to Key Largo and I thought, "Finally, I've found the guy to go cruising with." We started saving our money and fixing the boat up to go cruising. We decided we would plan for six months and if we could find work in the Caribbean we would keep going.

I was so excited because he could do anything on a boat. We worked hard together for six months preparing the boat and finally we were ready to leave. He fixed, repaired and replaced so many things to make sure my boat was safe and in good working order.

"If adventures are created from faux pas then my adventure has just begun!" That was the first line I wrote in my journal on December 4, 1999, the day we finally left Fort Lauderdale. Imagine being in a twenty-eight foot boat, seven miles off shore when you discover water gushing from the quarter berth.

Our first week out was similar to our first day even though I made sure we did not leave on a Friday, which is supposed to bring bad luck. Our week included things like: taking on water, the bilge pump malfunctioning, getting seasick, running aground, getting cuts and bruises, running out of fuel, the engine dying in the middle of the Gulf Stream, fuel filters clogging, and twenty-five knot winds blowing while we were anchored on the banks in the middle of nowhere. And he supposedly knew what he was doing!

Now some real problems began to arise between us. When you throw two people who don't know each other very well 24/7 into a small boat, the learning curve goes up. You quickly find out what people are made of and how they are wired. For example, on one of our night crossings, I was worried about a ship because I couldn't tell if it was on a collision course or not. There were at least half dozen ships off of Miami, and I started to panic. I woke him up to help me and he got angry with me. He told me I was, "freaking out." Sometimes women do that when they don't know what is going on. Instead of helping me he just got annoyed and then went back to bed.

My goal on this trip was to learn as much as possible. I knew there was a lot I didn't know. It was the stuff that I knew I didn't know that worried me the most. I wanted to learn how to make the right decisions, but I also wanted this to be a team effort. I wanted to discuss decisions first. I couldn't understand it when he started getting annoyed and talking down to me. We started arguing about decisions—about which way to go, about this and about that. It started to get petty and I grew tired of the arguing. By the time we got to Bimini and started to make our way across the banks, I was ready to call it quits. He would get irritated with me and we would start arguing again.

Everyone who's gone across the banks for the first time agrees that it is nerve-wracking to say the least. You are often in only in seven or eight feet of water. Thinking that you are going to run aground every few minutes takes its toll after a while. I would start panicking. Didier sat on the bow watching me zigzag around the dark spots in the water that I thought were shoals. Finally, he came back and took the helm and showed me that I was worried about nothing. You don't know what you don't know, but without a clear explanation it becomes conflict. At one point I turned the boat around and said, "We are going back because I don't want to do all this fighting." We managed to talk it out and turned back and kept going.

We then spent a hellish night on the banks when the winds and seas kicked up and we had no protection. There were five boats out on the banks that night. I found out later that all the women on the other boats had talked about catching the next plane out after that horrible night. My problem was that I couldn't leave because it was my boat!

Didier and I spent the next several weeks making our way down to Georgetown, Exuma. Every time we sailed together we would argue. When we would get to the anchorage, I would try to find out why we were having so many arguments. Each time he would give me a different reason. It wasn't until much later when I started doing my research on gender differences that I finally understood all the dynamics going on between us and working against us.

By the time we arrived in Georgetown, we were both ready to call it quits. I told him if he didn't want to be there he should leave. He took it as an ultimatum and said he would leave. I started to panic, because I had lost my confidence and I wasn't sure I could cruise by myself such a long way from home. On the flip side, I didn't want to go back, especially with my tail between my legs. I had enough money and provisions to keep me going for months. I thought, "Why should I go back just because he wants to?"

I started talking with some people at the anchorage. A guy who was single-handing his boat reassured me that I could do this. I knew that I had my brother, a retired Coast Guard Chief Quartermaster and accomplished sailor, who would come to my rescue if I really needed it.

With all this in mind, I told Didier that if he was going to leave, he would go alone. He told me he did not think I could do it on my own. That really made me angry! I thought to myself, "Well, now I have to prove that I can do this." That's when the real lessons began for me. We had only completed one month of our six-month plan to cruise to the Caribbean. Now here I was an instant single-hander, three hundred fifty miles from home. I looked forward to the challenge after being told I could not do it, but the truth is that I was also scared to death.

Cß

During the time I cruised alone, I experienced nights on the hook with gale force winds, encounters with tankers in the night while I was anchored too close to a channel, a collision between my boat and another boat at anchor at 2:00 in the morning, swamped dinghies, problems with batteries and problems with my electrical systems. I learned quickly how to maintain my engine, change filters and bleed the engine. Sailing in the Bahamas also included sailing with other women on my boat and teaching them how to sail and navigate. Teaching others gave me the assurance that I did know what I was doing.

One of the most unexpected realizations was that I suddenly found myself a social outcast when I became the only female single-hander in the anchorage. The scariest time was when I injured my back. This prevented me from being able to lift my anchor for almost a month. I never knew if anyone would be there to help me. There were tears and fears and then getting on with it and somehow getting through it.

Not all of it was bad. Many fun things happened too. I enjoy my memories of lobster for dinner, dolphins swimming around my boat, parties, dancing the Bahamian Rake & Scrape with Hugh McCall, the retired CEO of Bank of America and meeting other rich men who flew into Georgetown.

I was challenged with things like having to fight my way through the Dotham Cut with opposing current in twenty-five knot winds. It was certainly a challenge to avoid being pushed onto the rocks from the big washing machine-like waves as I came through the narrow cut.

I was able to overcome the challenge of pulling my anchor up after a sleepless night in those same twenty to twenty-five knot winds. At first I did not know how I would achieve this but I knew I had to leave this anchorage because I was on a lee shore and it would be worse to stay.

I survived one of my worst fears when I left Nassau, crossing the tongue of the ocean alone. With my autopilot broken, I spent the day at the helm, unable to leave, with no food or water for seven hours. When

faced with adversity, questioning one's very existence is common. Wondering if I would make it back alive kept me thinking and reviewing my life, my goals and my obtuse decision to risk my life doing such a crazy thing like sailing alone. Who would even know where I was or come to help? It had been hours since I had seen another boat. This was just crazy but I was committed. The only thing to do was to just keep going, and eventually, I made it.

My journey was completed with my single-handing Tididi, the 350 miles back to Fort Lauderdale, safely. I DID IT! (Incidentally, after seeing what I had accomplished on my own, Didier wanted me back.)

I had been shouted at by my dad and intimidated and glared at by Jack, but after the incessant arguments with Didier, I came back with a determination to find answers. Why couldn't we just get along? Why was I made to feel so small and incapable? Why did some couples seem to get along so easily while others bickered constantly? What was the secret to successful sailing partnerships? I simply had to know, and what I discovered I will now share with you.

TWO

LOOKING FOR ANSWERS & SOLUTIONS

You always hear about it when a woman is abandoning ship and leaving her husband. The quest for me was to find the reason some relationships work and some don't.

If you have done any cruising at all, or been around the boating community, you have either heard about or probably met a couple or two who have ended up at the point of parting company. And you might have even heard of a few of them ending in divorce. You may have met a guy who sailed to the location with his buddies because his wife refused to do the passage. She shows up once he survives the passage. She is willing to fly in after they make what was, in her mind, the bad part of the trip. Of course, it was the highlight of the trip in his mind.

How many single-hander, married men have you met out cruising or in your sailing club? Most often that is the guy who has either scared his wife so much that she will never return to the boat, or the guy who never learned to help his wife develop an appreciation for the sailing lifestyle. My apologies to the few men to whom these generalizations don't apply!..

Everyone who has been cruising will tell you of the couples they saw, or rather, heard, in the anchorage yelling and cursing at each other.

There are also entertaining scenes on the dock, but hopefully you are not on the wrong side of it. It is as embarrassing and humiliating for the spectators as it is for the entertainers. We all know of the couple yelling at each other coming into the anchorage. We hear the words being said and know quite a bit about them before they ever politely come over in their dinghy to introduce themselves. Did they forget how well water carries sound?

After Didier left, I went on a quest to determine the reasons why some couples survive together and even thrive together when others don't make it at all. Sailing alone in the Bahamas had its advantages and one was having the chance to interview other couples and ask them why they thought their relationship worked. I was on a mission to find out how a couple aboard can overcome the issues that cause conflict. But also, I wondered, "What were the things that kept women from becoming more accomplished? And why is it so difficult for women to become confident sailors? Can they really learn this stuff? Why does it seem so much easier for men than some women?"

Having had plenty of my own experiences on boats now, both good and bad, I realized that I could survive, and that, actually, all those experiences together are what it took to become an accomplished sailor. I know this is the last thing a woman wants to hear. We don't want to experience adversity or danger; we just want to know we will get home again safely. I know what it takes for women to be willing to make that leap of faith with their spouse. When men come to the realization that women really are different and need different things, then there can be harmony on the waves of life.

I know there are skeptics among you who are saying that there are no gender differences. I will address those doubts later. A confidential note to the cynical sailor: you may not always like what you hear, but if you remain open-minded and just try to apply some of my suggestions, you might get your partner onboard with your dreams of sailing the seven seas .

Unfortunately, there are those insecure males who feel threatened by a confident female. She may actually expose him to be an impostor. It wouldn't hurt him to have the cockiness taken down a few notches.

An over-blown ego in either sex is unbecoming and can get one into real trouble. If you are one of those types of people, this book may not be for you.

✿

My pursuits were partly selfish:, I wanted to figure out what went wrong with my relationship. What could I have done differently? Whose fault was it? Or was it anyone's fault? I knew there was a language barrier with French being Didier's first language, but why didn't we make it work despite that difficulty?

You always hear about it when a woman is abandoning ship and leaving her husband. Some fly back to the states for a time, and some for good. I knew I wasn't the only one with relationship problems, I was just the only woman willing to stay aboard alone. I could have turned around and returned to Florida with him, but I needed to know—for me, not anybody else—that I could sail my boat by myself .

Now after spending years teaching couples, reading books on gender differences and helping numerous couples work together, not only in teaching them how to sail, but how to work together as a team; I hope others can benefit from what I discovered as they consider what they will need when sailing together.

I can say with reasonable certainty that somewhere near ninety percent of people out cruising are couples, meaning only two people on a boat together. That means that Mars and Venus have to learn to live, work and survive together in a very small space. Furthermore, they are dependent on each other 24/7 for survival, for companionship, and for fun. They are also technically sailing short-handed since long passages require that both people get to sleep eventually. And if one person is asleep that means that the person left on deck is single-handing.

Everyone onboard needs to know what to do because of the possibility of someone getting injured, or worse, going overboard. It makes sense that both people know how to handle the boat under any and every circumstance and especially in emergencies.

So how do we make it work? How do we keep from having those

ridiculous arguments? Why does it work for some and not so well for others? Sometimes we need to put that ego away and be concerned more for the other person than ourselves. I see a similar thread running through all the couples that have taken my sailing classes. They are taking the class, usually at his initiation, because he is concerned about her needs and her happiness. He wants to make sure that she knows he is there for her, even though he may not be certain what her needs are. What great guys—I wish I could clone them!

He is also a very smart man, because he knows that if he doesn't help her enjoy sailing, then he doesn't get to realize his dream. Smart men want their mates to become proficient in life-saving skills, since he may someday be the beneficiary! Remember that Coast Guard statistics show that eighty percent of all man-over-board rescues are men with their zippers down. It is called MAN overboard (MOB) for a reason !

In the next pages we will explore gender differences—things to consider because of the way he is wired verses the way she is wired—and how those differences affect how we learn, process and communicate and, lastly, how to do it all in harmony.

Because I am a woman, I will, of course, offer the woman's perspective, but I will also discuss the differences between that perspective and the man's.. I am also coming from the perspective of a trainer so I will talk a lot about teaching others.

DISCLAIMER

It's a shame that I should even have to include such a thing as a disclaimer in a book, but I know how sensitive some people can be. Ever notice how it's often people who are guilty of the offense that get offended? So to make sure that I am not being misquoted or misinterpreted I will make clear my intentions. I will be addressing sensitive matters such as gender bias and discrimination.

I want to make clear that this is not at all a book about bashing men. I have, in fact, gained a greater appreciation, respect and admiration for men as a result of my quest to find out what went wrong in my

own relationships and learn about gender differences ., But I will tell you that I have no respect for anyone who treats women as second-class citizens or who thinks women are any less capable. And I do not tolerate anyone who is disrespectful to me on my boat or who treats me with disrespect when I am on his or her boat. The policy on my boat is to stop everything and go below when someone starts yelling.

So guys and gals, please understand that in discussing these differences you should keep in the back of your mind that I will do some generalizing to emphasize the differences and I apologize in advance to anyone who may be offended. I truly mean no offense to anyone, either male or female. My purposes are not to stereotype, but to emphasize the point.

I can also tell you that while I operate very much as most women do on land, my inclinations are more masculine than feminine when I am on the boat. I'm not really a tomboy-type and I don't want to be masculine; I like being feminine in every aspect and even wear lipstick even when I'm sailing! I endeavor to maintain my femininity, while still being strong, confident and capable on a boat. I have no problem admitting my weaknesses and shortcomings when it comes to working on engines and trying to loosen a tight bolt. There is a delicate balance between being confident and capable and still being the person that we are. As a woman, I really don't want to take on the typically "blue duties" of working in the bilges and engines. But I'm happy and confident in sharing the responsibilities. I want to know enough about the engine so that I can either help or take care of things when necessary. But I really don't want to have the day-to-day engineering responsibilities, or to do troubleshooting for problems . I believe that we should all utilize our strengths, whether typically "pink" or "blue."

When I am on someone else's boat, I am always respectful even when I don't agree. The right way is ALWAYS the Captain's way, without exception, when you are sailing on someone else's boat. It is always the crew's responsibility to obey and not to argue. The law says that there must always be a designated captain and it doesn't always have to be the guy. I believe that it should be a team effort, but I'm getting ahead of myself .

Let's also be clear before we even get started, I'm not here to say that one gender is better or worse than the other. I don't even claim to be an expert on this topic, but I will share with you what I found by doing research and listening to the experts. Then I will share a combination of my own experiences and the patterns I observed in the many couples that I have sailed with and taught over the years.

This book is about creating a mutual, positive playing field between the two genders. We need to be okay with the differences in who we are and how we learn. You may not always agree or relate with some of the characteristics, but it doesn't mean that they aren't part of the typical masculine or feminine genetic makeup. It just means that they are not a part of you personally, and that's okay too.

Please keep an open mind and be willing to consider, ponder, and ask questions before you make judgment . Just because you learn one particular way, does not mean that everyone learns the same way you do.

We will be discussing many characteristics documented by numerous credentialed professionals, many of whom have spent years observing the behaviors of children and adults in a variety of circumstances. Probably the most popular and widely recognized expert on this subject is Dr. John Gray, Ph.D., author of a series of books called Men Are From Mars and Women Are From Venus. I will not attempt to go as in-depth as Dr. Gray, so I highly recommend his books and others listed in the Bibliography for further reading .

THREE

NOT GOOD, NOT BAD, JUST DIFFERENT

If you are a sailor and have ever used your engine, you should not be so quick to judge a power boater.

UNDERSTANDING EACH OTHER'S PERSPECTIVE

I would like you to take a little quiz . Don't worry—there is no passing or failing involved, just thinking.

Question one: which is better, an apple or an orange? Is one bad and the other good? Or are they just different? Maybe you prefer apples, so you say oranges are bad. No, I think we can agree that fruit is good and people have different preferences. Okay, let's put it in sailing terms.

Question two: which is better, monohulls or multihulls? There are those who prefer the monohull and others, the multihull. Is it the multihull that's bad because you sail a monohull? Which is good and which is bad? Do you agree that they are just different? I think we are making progress here.

Question three: what kind of boat is best, power or sail? Oh, I might have a few of you on this one. I might have you backed into a corner if you are one of those die-hard sailors. We have talked about each other enough. Power boaters call sailors rag-sailors and sail boaters call power boaters stink-potters. So which are good and which are bad?

Two on a Boat How to Keep it Afloat

I remember walking down the dock in Seattle and this older man approached me. He gave me his business card and asked me to call him. I asked him if he had a boat. He said, "Yes." So I inquired if it was power or sail? He said, "Power." I told him that he would not be hearing from me. At the time, I was completely sold on the sailboat experience. But since then, I have traveled to Europe from Antigua to Copenhagen on a one hundred sixty-two foot mega power-yacht and I have to tell you, it was a blast! Being on the water can be great in any kind of boat. (Although I admit that I'm still not excited about those loud cigarette boats!)

For those sailors who are so confident that they are right, (after all, we were green before going green was popular), I have one question. Do you have an engine in your boat? Do you have one on the stern or maybe an outboard for your dinghy? Would you agree that power has its place on the water? If you are a sailor and have ever used your engine, you should not be so quick to judge a power boater.

And for those of you without sails, what would you give to have a sail when the engine dies or you run out of gas and are stuck bobbing on the water for hours waiting for help? So maybe sails can be helpful, too.

Then both power and sail have good and bad points, if you want to put it that way. It's more that they are just different and each has its place in the world. Variety is the spice of life, after all.

Last Question: true or false, everyone must be just like me or else there is something wrong with them? My ex-husband was convinced that there was something wrong with me. However, after reading John Gray's book, Men are from Mars and Women from Venus, I realized that the only thing wrong with me was that I was a woman. I acted and thought and responded like a woman, like most women do. So the thing that was wrong with me was that I was not a man.

How about if I said everyone must be a monohull boater or I will not associate with him or her in my club. If you are not like me you must be a bad person and if you don't change I won't like you. Does this sound absurd?

How did you do on the quiz? If you answered honestly that two things can be different without one being "bad" and the other "good," then you are ready to see that this is how we must begin to look at gender differences. Men and women make different contributions which create a balance between the genders.

Not good, not bad... just different.

TWO ON A BOAT HOW TO KEEP IT AFLOAT

FOUR

RESOLVING WOMEN'S RESERVATIONS & APPREHENSIONS IN SAILING

"I don't know why we bother taking them when they're so much trouble!" —He says, somewhat jokingly, after reading the following list of women's issues and concerns.

Why is it, then, that we want to change our partners? If he were a woman would you have wanted to marry him? If she had chest hair would you find her more attractive? You are probably saying, Josie, you are being ridiculous. Of course I am. My point is that desiring to make you just like me is ridiculous. In other words, to say that you need to think, act or make decisions like me is unreasonable. As partners, you chose each other for those differences, and now you want that person to change to be more like you—does this make sense? We need to learn to embrace those differences by first understanding them and then being willing to say it's okay to be different. Once you recognize your partner's differences, hopefully you can learn to accept and appreciate them and approach your partner in a new way that will allow each of you to be, unapologetically, your own person.

Please keep in mind I am not an expert on gender, by any means. From the many experts out there, though, you can be sure that what I am conveying is not just a figment of my imagination. There have been years of research on human behavior.

I do believe that insecurity and lack of confidence work against any relationship, as could be seen even between myself and other women who felt threatened by me while I was single-handing. Several women admitted to me later, after they had gotten to know me, that they didn't like me at first because they felt intimidated. For me, that was a difficult pill to swallow, because, as women, we really need that connection to each other.

What I accomplished as a single-hander was done out of necessity, not to prove myself superior to anyone. I am not a competitive person by nature. I was not racing on boats or thinking of setting any records. I just wanted to prove to myself that I could do anything I set my mind to.

There is a big majority of women in boating today who are not interested in racing. They are not into that whole competitive thing. The only reason I did any racing was because it was the only way to get a ride on a boat sometimes. I don't mind doing it, if it is just for fun, but I don't want all that yelling going on when I'm on the water. It's not what motivates me to sail.

I think it's important for people cruising to keep an open mind towards others and their abilities. And sometimes, lack of abilities. We all have something to contribute to make a better world.

There are quite a few men who would be considered feminine or "weak" because they don't know the first thing about mechanics and boat systems. They are just as helpless as most women if something major goes wrong when out sailing. It's not something to look down upon; it's just the differences in strengths and abilities. Very often I would hear the wives calling on the cruisers net asking for help, because the husband's pride would not allow him to admit that he needed help. Women usually don't have a problem with asking for help.

So let's look at these differences, knowing that even within our gender role we may exhibit various traits and characteristics typical of the other. Remember: this is not about who is good or bad or who is right or wrong. You may recognize things that are considered a "pink" or "blue" trait, but even as we label them, we must be careful avoid the extremes of always and never. By keeping an open mind you should begin to recognize specific gender attributes in yourself and in your partner. Explore these qualities together so that you can help each other, appreciate each other and enjoy your time together aboard your boat in a more positive and supportive way.

SURVEY RESULTS ON 20 CONFIDENCE KILLERS

Over the last few years I have been surveying women on my web site and at boat shows, my sailing students and women who boat or live aboard. The following are the responses compiled from approximately three hundred women who completed this survey. I started taking the survey because I had so many women inquire about taking sailing classes, but very few who actually followed through. I was curious as to why they were not attending classes even though they had expressed interest.

Most women are comforted when they see that an issue affecting them is common to others. A woman needs to know that it is not all "in her mind." So ladies, you can take comfort that you are not alone when it comes to the feelings you have when out on the water, especially when you first start out.

Some of the responses in the survey did not surprise me. I know from personal experience how women feel about being yelled at or the boat heeling. What astonished me about the survey was just how many issues hold women back from the attempt at becoming confident on the water. Most women would check three, four, or five and sometimes as many as ten of these issues that they felt were barriers to their becoming competent boaters. You will see that many of the issues are related. For instance, where there is lack of understanding—not getting how the wind works, for example—boat-handling confidence will be undermined, because what is not understood is often feared .

I perceive that these issues are not being discussed or dealt with in a realistic way. There are just too many women going sailing with their concerns and fears always lying just under the surface, waiting to emerge and wreak havoc when a stressful situation occurs. These anxieties are either being minimized or dismissed by a sailing partner who thinks of them only as "women's issues," as if these feelings are not real or valid since only women seem to have them. In reality, while men may actually share these same issues, most will never talk about them. A man may simply avoid a situation that makes him uncomfortable. I have met quite a few men who don't like the boat heeled over too much; maybe that is why some of them end up on powerboats!

Women have repeatedly said to me, "I just do what I'm told." It seems so sad to me that someone would be trapped in a subservient mentality simply because they have never mastered basic sailing skills. Not knowing or understanding your environment is one of the biggest causes of fear. When you learn to control your environment, you will have many of your fears under control, too. This theme runs through much of the following pages: one must have a strong foundation on which to build sailing skills. For you ladies who struggle, I have developed a whole program to help women learn the wind and understand the basics of sailing; this will be discussed at length in a later chapter. To the guys who know the concerns of your mate, you can be supportive in a variety of ways to help her overcome them and become accomplished sailors. So let's look at these issues one by one and figure out some solutions.

1. SHE DOESN'T WANT TO BE YELLED AT (84%)

Is anyone surprised that this is the number one objection that women have? Even men tell me they don't want to be yelled at, so what is all this yelling about? It appears that although everyone knows this is a problem, nothing is changing and women simply leave boating to the men in order to avoid being yelled at.

Until the yellers and yell-ees learn to communicate better , the problems will never go away. Unfortunately, what generally happens is that a person goes away instead. Let's take a look at what is really going on and get everything on the table. Remember, this is a two-way street. So there are things that both people can do differently to resolve this.

There are times on a boat when it is very important to raise your voice. And then there are others when that kind of communication is completely ineffective. There just isn't any time that I can think of when belittling others or using foul language is necessary or motivating. It is better to bite your tongue and walk away than to say something that you will regret. A whole chapter is devoted to this topic alone since it seems to eclipse all other concerns.

Women can be more proactive and decide what they are willing to tolerate. Set your boundaries, ladies! Tell the person who is yelling at you that you are not comfortable with his or her language. If it continues, remove yourself from that environment. You can do that temporarily by going below decks and then once back on land where you are safe, get away. Don't go back to a verbal abuser unless you are a glutton for punishment. Let the person know that it is simply unacceptable to speak to you disrespectfully.

If you are in a class environment with an instructor who yells, tell the person that you are not comfortable or talk to his boss without delay. Sometimes people have stern or loud voices that can be misinterpreted. Although men often have more commanding voices, they are not that the only ones whose tone can be misunderstood. Being Italian, and coming from a large family, I learned to talk loudly in order to be heard. My talking loudly to a soft-spoken person can be misinterpreted. There is a difference between needing to be heard and yelling angrily. See the chapter on yelling to learn the distinction between being yelled at and being yelled to.

The number one comment that I get from men when I talk about guys yelling is that they usually yell when they themselves don't know what they are doing. Wow—that was enlightening! There must be some truth to it .

Have you ever noticed that some people, when they meet a blind person or someone who does not speak English, start talking louder and slower, thinking that somehow a higher volume will make the other person see or understand? Louder does not make the words change. It may be comical to watch, but I feel sorry for the blind person, who will hopefully inform the yeller that they can hear just fine!

Sometimes people think that speaking louder will convey meaning where communication skills fail them. Instead, changing the words and putting things in a different way makes a world of difference for the person who is trying to understand. I have caught myself before getting frustrated when trying to make myself understood, and have been successful at helping students understand me by just rewording the information. There was no need to yell.

Using the right terminology helps too. To the experienced sailor: don't use layman's terms with new people. Get them understanding and using the right language from the beginning (a line is not a rope, the head is a bathroom, etc.), but don't expect them to understand if you don't first explain the language.

2. SHE DOESN'T UNDERSTAND THE WIND (57%)

Since understanding the wind is the foundation of sailing, if you don't get this down, you won't understand anything else in the sailing environment. When you understand the wind, you can make good, safe and informed decisions. Confidence in this subject alone can make or break a person's whole experience on a boat.

You cannot expect to know how to dock a boat, turn the right direction, do a M.O.B. maneuver, control your boat, or make it go where you want it to go if you don't understand the wind. You cannot know how to stop a boat for docking, anchoring or picking up a mooring, if you don't know from which direction the wind is coming. All decisions begin with knowing wind direction and strength.

Because men "see" or conceptualize the wind differently than women, it can be impossible for her to learn this from a guy. This was my problem for years—I did not understand what he meant when he said, "Head up!" When he would say, "Don't you see it up there on the bow?" I was thinking, "How do you see something that is invisible?"

Learning the wind allows us to control our environment, and by controlling our environment we have power over our safety, and that is one of the most important things for women. I will never forget the "Ah-ha!" moment when I finally understood what was going on. Suddenly, everything on the boat changed for me. Learn the wind, and that which

has caused fear becomes a pleasure and a thrilling challenge. See the chapter on the wind or look into my online live training sessions if you struggle with this topic, because I believe that women can learn this very easily when taught in their mode of learning.

Most of the issues contained in this chapter could be resolved if this subject alone were properly addressed. When women understand the foundation of sailing and learn how to see and feel the invisible wind, they can accomplish anything! I have often seen women who have been sailing for years finally understand the wind for the first time out sailing with me. They experience success the first time because of the method by which they are learning, and it works for everyone, both men and women.

3. SHE DOESN'T WANT TO BE CRITICIZED (54%)

It's not surprising that this subject is near the top. Yelling is bad enough, but when it is coupled with derogatory comments or profanity, it will cause most people to just shut down. I come by this information first-hand.

Most people will either mentally or emotionally withdraw when talked to in an insulting or abusive manner. Their willingness to participate diminishes or completely disappears. They shut down their mind to learning and they shut down to the person who is making the insulting comments. This can include those looks of annoyance and frustration that say so much. Sometimes the non-verbal communication can cut worse than the verbal comments. Anything that hurts someone is inappropriate, but even more so in a learning environment. In a future chapter, I talk more about inappropriate communication.

I have had men aboard my boat in classes who were uncooperative and threatening in their demeanor to me personally. I know my strengths and weaknesses and I take a passive stance in an environment where I do not feel safe. Remember, your safety is always a priority. Once in a safe place, take the necessary steps to protect yourself and get away from an abusive person.

4. SHE FEARS STORMS OR TOO MUCH WIND (51%)

Believe it or not, there are many simple preparations that you can make to help you avoid ninety-five percent of the bad weather. Pre-planning and taking one's time can save a lot of fear and heartache. Don't wait until the last minute, when you see those dark clouds coming. Too many people are fooled by storms coming from an unexpected direction. A good weather-training program can teach you how to understand and interpret the weather so that this becomes a non-issue for you.

Lee Chesneau, a meteorologist who has years of experience in marine weather, does training courses specifically for cruisers. His book, Heavy Weather Avoidance and Route Design has helped captains of major shipping companies avoid the worst conditions. All cruisers should try to become their own weather experts. At bare minimum you need to learn how to read weather faxes and understand clouds so you can make good, informed decisions. As the book says, "avoidance" is the best plan.

Some people in my classes get angry or disappointed when they don't get to go sailing, but I would rather disappoint them than scare them to death. Here in Florida, the lightning capital of the country, a single thunderstorm can have over a thousand lighting strikes, so I just don't take any chances. A good rule is if it looks like the weather is not cooperating, don't make commitments that will place you in harm's way.

Learning to trust your instincts is also really important. The rule of thumb on reefing, or reducing sail, is: If you think you need to reef, then you need to reef. Better to shake out a reef than to be caught in the strong winds with too much sail up.

Sooner or later, if you sail long enough, you will be caught in a storm. So although avoidance works most of the time, being prepared and knowing what to do must come first. This begins with building your foundation and understanding the wind and weather. When we know what to look for, and how to respond, we can handle what is put in front of us in an intelligent and controlled way. This equates to safety at sea.

5. SHE WORRIES THAT SHE WON'T KNOW WHAT TO DO (47%)

In a stressful situation, when we aren't sure which is the right thing to do, we may feel fear and even paralysis. The bottom line here: go back to the basics. If you haven't learned the basics of sailing and how to control your boat, of course you are not going to know what to do when a crisis occurs. The problem is that what we don't know can hurt us!

I have a difficult time comprehending how people can spend thousands of dollars getting a boat ready to sail and go cruising, making sure she is seaworthy and water-tight, getting the right instruments and charts, books and gear, but then neglect the most important part of preparation—themselves! Why wouldn't everyone take the time to learn skills that can save their lives? You wouldn't want a doctor who didn't finish medical school to perform brain surgery on you. So don't expect to go out and challenge the elements in a tiny boat without first preparing yourself.

It is possible to read books about sailing but not know how to do it. Basic concepts can be learned by reading, but who wants to find gaps in knowledge in the midst of the storm? No wonder women are often scared to death; she is dependant on someone who is flying by the seat of his pants. So many boats get sold after the first voyage because people get into a serious situation for which they are not properly prepared and which causes a lot of trouble. Ladies (and gentlemen), you are worth the money it costs to take sailing classes. Don't underestimate your worth and don't assume that you can just rely on your partner to do and know it all. It's your life, and you are responsible for your own well-being.

I would guess that probably seventy-five to eighty percent of the women who take my sailing classes tell me, "I read the book but didn't really understand it." I was one of those women. I could not just read it and do it. Like many women, I am a visual and hands-on learner. Once you do things on the water like raising sails and learning how to make a boat move or stop, then it is much easier to go back and read it again to solidify the information. Most women tell me something like, "You can talk about it until you are blue in the face but until I do it, I really just don't get it."

You will never overcome the fear of doing the wrong thing until you get out there in the right learning environment and practice. Start with a friend you trust, or take a one or two-day class—something to begin the process. I have a network of professional women captains and instructors that I work with throughout the country; there is no good excuse for not taking a class, seminar or clinic somewhere and in some capacity. Now you can even do online seminars that will get you started. They are affordable—isn't your life is worth it?

6. SHE CAN'T REMEMBER NAMES OF THINGS (45%)

If I go to France and everyone is speaking French, I can't possibly communicate if I don't first take the time to learn the language. Sailing has its own language. You cannot expect yourself or anyone else to step onto a boat and understand what's going on without knowing the vocabulary. Learning jargon is the first part of understanding any new subject. Again, you can get a book for starters, but it really helps to spend time on a boat to put the knowledge to practical use.

I really believe that sailing is very logical; when you learn in an orderly way you will remember the material much more easily. That is why I keep it as simple as possible, using the K. I. S. S. method– Keep It Simple, Sweetheart! Also, you do yourself a disservice when you try to just memorize things. You don't own the information if you just learn by rote. If you want to move something to long term memory, you've got to use it and it has to become a part of you.

7. SHE DOESN'T KNOW HOW TO DOCK THE BOAT (45%)

This is a topic that affects both men and women, and keeps many boats in their slips instead of out sailing. Ladies, you are not alone in

feeling nervous!

This topic is also related to understanding the wind. How can you possibly know how to properly dock the boat if you don't understand how the wind and current are affecting you? There are about a dozen factors you need to consider when leaving the dock and returning to the slip, yet we only hold three things in our short-term memory. How can you become accomplished unless you learn the factors so well that you begin to consider them automatically? Without understanding how the wind works, you cannot know how to read it and anticipate what it will do. The current can be even more dangerous if you don't know what you are looking for and how your boat will react and respond.

Docking is a learned skill that comes with practice. And guess what is the first thing that you will need to ask yourself? Right—where is the wind? So, if you have not built your house by starting with the solid foundation of understanding the invisible wind, how do you expect those experiences to turn out?

The purpose of my career is to help people to become a success, so rather than having people merely memorize information for a test, I teach the thought processes going on behind the scenes. What things do we need to think about and consider so that we can make good decisions? Sometimes our first plan doesn't work out and then we must reconsider the decision and be able to change course, sometimes in an instant. What is the "plan B" when "plan A" is falling apart? What is the worst-case scenario, and how would we respond if it were to happen? Yes, I know, it's a lot to think about, but our problem is that "we don't know what we don't know." So we need someone to teach it to us before we find ourselves in the stressful situation.

8. SHE IS AFRAID OF THE BOAT HEELING OVER TOO MUCH (40%)

Can you see where this is going yet? This is yet another issue that stems from not knowing the basic foundation of sailing—understanding the invisible wind.

For those with a racing mentality, sailing is about the excitement of putting the rail in the water, but actually, anything more than about a fifteen degree heel creates leeway that makes the boat sail inefficiently. You may feel like you are sailing faster, but because the boat is slipping sideways rather than following a more direct route, it will actually take longer to get to the destination. It may be counter intuitive, but the boat is not going to lose speed when you reef, but rather sail more efficiently and comfortably, too. Only when you have eight "deck monkeys" sitting on the high side of the boat helping to balance it, can rail in the water work for boat speed! This is an unlikely situation when two of you are out for a leisurely sail. Putting in a reef or easing the mainsail so that the boat is not over-powered makes both the boat and mama happy. So why wouldn't a guy do that for both his girls?

Most women will overcome their fear of the boat heeling by understanding the dynamics of sailing and learning how to control the boat. I can't tell you how many times I have had a woman on the boat that couldn't even begin the first sailing lesson because she was so afraid of the boat heeling too much. It has always been my policy to keep the boat at no more than a ten degree heel while teaching. It puts a woman at ease so that her mind can focus on what she is learning, rather than anticipating what bad thing might happen next.

I hear so often the stories of women who have been taken out in too much wind and are now petrified to get back on a boat. In a training setting, this goes beyond disrespect toward a student, particularly because it often took all her courage just to step on the boat in the first place. It's critically important that women find a supportive instructor so that they can overcome their fears. The worst thing a woman can do is end up with one of those "old school" male instructors who thinks that there is either something wrong with women because they can't learn it or yells at you when you don't get it. (See more in the chapter on Gender Bias.)

It's very important for women who are sensitive to any of these issues to find another woman from whom to learn. It's not that there aren't any great male teachers and instructors out there; I know there are because many are good friends of mine, with whom I have trained and also have watched train other women. It's just that you really have to do your homework to find them. However, for those women who are sensitive, have already had bad experiences, or who simply want to start with good experiences, I still recommend learning from another woman because she is more likely to understand their needs.

9. SHE DOESN'T WANT TO GIVE UP CREATURE COMFORTS (29%)

There are some people who are okay with roughing it, but the majority of women would prefer to keep at least some creature comforts. I personally am not willing to give up my toilet and hot shower, thank you very much. Do I need to sit in the lap of luxury on a the million-dollar yacht? Maybe not. I can live without an electric macerator, but I do have my hot water hooked up to the engine so that by the time I motor into the anchorage, I can take a hot shower if I want.

I did go from thinking that a forty-four foot boat was too small, to actually living for seven years on a twenty-eight foot boat. So what does that tell you? I learned how to live smaller over time, and how to adjust my expectations gradually, figuring out what I was willing to give up and what I was not.

I still don't want to sail on a boat without a dodger so I can get out of the wind, the rain, the sun or the cold. I would prefer a boat with a full cockpit enclosure if given the option. Do you need a television or microwave? Or would you be happier with a book? I've done without luxury items, and I've also been on boats with all the amenities. The seventy-foot sailboat, Maya, lacked nothing. It even had a bread machine! While there is nothing like the aroma of bread that basically baked itself, it may be something you can live without. But with some things you just can't compromise; things like water and keeping dry are not luxuries, they are necessities.

I think there is a very easy resolution to the questions about comfort. If the guy wants to spend thousands of dollars on new instruments, gadgets and the like, then he can buy one more toy for the boat, an inverter, an electric toilet or whatever it is that would make life easier for his mate. Add a couple more batteries and, voila! You have enough electricity for things like hair dryers. You don't necessarily have to give up your favorite electrical appliances—it may mean the ability to make a good cup of coffee or even an espresso.

One creature comfort that I think is an absolute must if you are going to be traveling to foreign countries is a water maker. A desalinator is not really a luxury if you can't find a good source of fresh water; it becomes a must! When we landed in Nuka Hiva in French Polynesia, we could not find even brackish water. Even if we could, brackish water can contaminate water tanks with local parasites. I got deathly ill after filling my tanks with water in Nassau. I've even heard of people's pets suddenly dying.

With all of the pink and blue duties, there should also be a his and hers wish list for the boat. Some items are mutually beneficial while others may seem like an extravagance to one's mate. She may not see the benefit of having an extra fuel filter, but will come to appreciate it if the fuel gets clogged and the engine dies while entering a channel. And he may not think that an electric toilet is necessary, but after repairing the joker valve for the third time in the hand-pump head, he may see her side of the argument .

10. SHE IS FEARFUL OF FEELING TRAPPED (28%)

I worried a lot about this issue when I thought about the possibility of crossing an ocean. I tried to imagine being out in the middle of the ocean for ten, twenty, even thirty days. What would I do? *What if* we sank? *What if* we started arguing and fighting, where would I go? How would I escape? The sheer amount of *what ifs* caused even more apprehension and discouraged me from doing such a long passage at all.

I can tell you after the fact that I have given up many an opportunity to sail to some great places because I felt like the guy's intentions were not honorable. I just didn't feel that I would be safe; or worse, I would be expected to do something that I didn't want to do. Like stay in his berth with the threat of "put out or get out and swim with the sharks."

I remember worrying about being out of sight of land. Going offshore meant no turning back and no escape. If I decided that I didn't like it, I was trapped, and that is pretty daunting. My astrological sign is Leo the Lion (a cat). Cats don't like to be cornered or trapped, so I saw being on a boat with no escape more like being in a cage than being free. Then I started dreaming of the possibilities and the adventures that would be in store. I listened to people who told their tales. The stories, the pictures and the people were the things that motivated and excited me and got me beyond my fear of the *what if*s..

I will share with you later the process I went through to go from landlubber to cruiser. I really bought into the dream of sailing to Tahiti. And now that I have been there, done that, I can say that I have had two absolutely fabulous ocean passages. And I would do it again should the opportunity arise.

11. SHE IS WORRIED ABOUT DOING M.O.B. DRILLS (25%)

By now you can see the pattern in the list of women's concerns, and this worry is no different. Without understanding the foundation of sailing, the wind, we cannot begin to understand how to get the boat turned around and back to our victim in the water. This has to be the most terrifying of thoughts for all of us. Those unknowns surface again. *What if* we are under sail rather than under power? Isn't it better to just turn on the engine? Can't I just call someone on the cell phone? Why can't he just swim back to me? *What if* he's unconscious?

If you don't know the answers to these questions, you had better figure them out before you set sail. For those who know how to sail, you might think that they are way off-base. But for those who don't know how to get a boat back to the victim, these questions may not be so crazy. We don't know what we don't know , and those unknowns can hurt or scare us and affect the person with whom we are sailing (especially if they end up in the water!).

So begin at the beginning. First, learn the wind, and then learn how to control the boat. Know how to tack and jibe, heave-to and stop a boat both under power and sail. You might be saying, "It doesn't sound like you're helping me much here, Josie." Well, I really am trying to help. Coast Guard statistics show that eighty percent of all real M.O.B. calls are rescuing men with their zippers down. Who's probably doing the rescue procedure here? And often with nobody else is on board to help!

Now you know why I don't call it "crew overboard" to be politically correct. I'm not interested in being politically correct; I'm interested in keeping people safe. I doubt very seriously that you hear of too many incidents of women peeing off the boat and falling in the water. Let's take a quick poll: Ladies, how many of you are willing to pee off the back of the boat? I thought so. I'm sure there are a few rebels out there, but most women will prefer privacy and safety. So the reality is that guys should be far more concerned about making sure their sailing partners know how to do a rescue, if they want to live to tell about it. Basic sailing skills and safety drills are necessary, not optional.

And to you ladies, you should be worried about this one. But don't just avoid it, do something about it. Fear should motivate, not paralyze you. Make sure that you do whatever it takes to know how to rescue others, and also to survive yourself.

I always suggest to my students that they purchase an inflatable life jacket with a harness. These babies run about two hundred fifty dollars at West Marine. The Bluestorm version sells for about one hundred eighty-five dollars on the womensailing.com web site. I mentioned the price to a couple on my boat. The husband was choking on the price of the jackets. I looked at him ready to ask, "What is your life worth?" However, with a slip of the tongue I asked him instead, "What is your wife worth?" It shut him up quicker than quick. It was funny how it came out but I have to ask you, "What is your life worth?" If you don't think your own life, or that of anyone else, is worth at least a couple hundred bucks, I'd say you have a problem.

We need to always be thinking about safety. Let's get our priorities straight here. Sailing is meant to be fun, so safety must always be the priority. People who get lax about this usually become a statistic. So sometimes fear is a good thing.

12. SHE IS WORRIED SHE WILL GET SEASICK (23%)

Seasickness affects everyone sooner or later. I know, you're thinking, "Here she goes again. You're not being much help, Josie." But let me finish.

I remember worrying about this when my boyfriend, Jack, would start saying to me, "I gotta' get you out in those ten foot seas." Of course, this just petrified me and it was not a great motivator to make me want to follow him across the South Pacific.

However, we had a good friend that Jack sailed a lot with, named John Guzzwell. John wrote a book called Trekka, after the name of his boat. John had built a twenty-seven foot wooden boat in the 1950's and then single-handed it around the world before there were GPS units, satellite phones, and internet access to weather. I will never forget John's response to me when I asked him if he ever got seasick. He said, "Josie, every time I make an ocean passage I get sea sick." I was shocked. How could anyone even want to go sailing again if they got seasick? He told me that he knew he would get sick, so he prepared for it. He would make his meals ahead of time, and just do the minimum until he got over it. Usually within a couple of days he was fine for the rest of the trip. You can read about it in his book.

So I decided that if John Guzzwell could do it, I would try and do it too. My first really rough passage was going from Fort Lauderdale to Bimini, Bahamas. It was really rough and I remember asking the guys how big the seas were. They thought we were experiencing eight foot seas.. I remembered all those times Jack would say, "I gotta' get you out in those ten foot seas." And here I was, close to it. It didn't seem so bad. At least I was not throwing my guts up. Even though I was queasy and very lethargic, I thought, "Hey, I did it!"

I found out that even queasiness is considered a mild form of seasickness. So the question is, what am I willing to put up with to accomplish the dream, the goal, and the adventure?

Now reality...being dizzy or nauseous is not fun and can make us miserable. It helps to know what causes the problem. Seasickness or motion sickness comes partly from the imbalances happening in our inner ear. There is fluid in the ear canal that balances us when we are in motion. When there is a conflict because of the boat moving up and down and back and forth, it causes our body to be out of balance. There are plenty of patches and seasick medicines on the market that work, if you take them ahead of time. I personally don't like a lot of them because they make you sleepy. You can make bad decisions when you are tired and not thinking clearly. I always suggest taking them at night and a day or two in advance to build up in your system. At a minimum, take the medicine the night before and get a good night's rest.

There are some very good natural remedies, like ginger, that help after you've already begun to feel queasy. I have also used the *Motion Eaze* liquid, which is all natural, with great success. I and one other woman were sailing my boat down to Miami. We were easily in five foot seas or more. She was at the helm and I was feeling sick. I dabbed the *Motion Eaze*, like perfume, behind my ears and sat quietly. It wasn't long, I would say less than 30 minutes, and I suddenly felt fine. I took the helm and never had a problem the rest of the trip.

If you feel sleepy, then sleep. Don't fight it. If you think you are going to throw up do it, you will feel better afterwards. Keeping something in the stomach, like crackers, helps too. For a lot of people being out on deck is better. I found most people are okay until they go below to use the head. By the time they come back up they are sick. Taking the helm and watching the horizon helps.

There are also acupressure bands you can buy. Some people swear by them and others don't believe they work. I don't know but I would try anything rather than nothing, or worse, letting seasickness keep me from an opportunity of a lifetime. Sometimes people use fear, the possibility of what may happen, as an excuse to avoid going out on the water altogether.

It's always good to plan and be properly prepared, in the event it happens. It happens to the best of us at one time or another. Also, remember that what we eat and drink the day before can certainly affect us. Getting dehydrated can affect us. Too much alcohol can affect us. Diesel fumes can affect us. I could go on and on.

My last word on the subject: the only time I have ever actually thrown up was when I was on the one-hundred-sixty-two-foot megapower yacht. So go figure!

13. SHE IS AFRAID OF LOSING SIGHT OF LAND (22%)

Being able to take multi-day trips was a step-by-step process for me. First, I would sail with my back to land every time I did a day sail. Then we did several overnight trips to the Bahamas and only one of those trips was stormy with big seas. I survived okay, so I started thinking that this idea might not be so bad after all.

Reality and perception play a big role when considering this fear How I personally overcame it was by taking small steps. When you are sailing south from Fort Lauderdale to Miami, and you sit on the starboard side of the boat, you are looking out into the Atlantic Ocean. All you see is water. I would purposely position myself with my back to land and try to imagine being out on the ocean without any land. I had the opportunity to make several trips to the Bahamas, and it doesn't take long to be out of sight of land when the land is as flat as Florida. So I would just ask myself, "What's the big deal?" And in the twenty-five days I was at sea sailing the South Pacific, it never was a big deal.

14. SHE THINKS SAILING CLASSES COST TOO MUCH (16%)

This goes back to my question, what is your life worth? What is too much when you look at the benefits of feeling safe, of understanding the wind and knowing the right things to do in times of crisis? Why is it we can spend thousands of dollars putting the biggest and best gadgets on the boat to make it sea-worthy and comfortable, but compromise when it comes to preparing ourselves?

Now I'm not putting down the classes on provisioning the boat and those types of tasks that women seem to fall into doing; but what is it going to take for women to realize that being prepared includes being prepared for any emergency? How many scary stories do you have to hear before you see that it could happen to you if you are not prepared. Remember Noah?

I really believe that women would be less fearful if they would prepare as if they are going to need to do this to save their own lives. On second thought, isn't that what we are supposed to be doing? If every person on the boat is not capable of at least navigating to safety, anchoring, reefing, heaving-to, performing M.O.B. drills under both power and sail and docking a boat, then you have not done all your prep work for heading off into the sunset.

Whether it is sailing to the Keys or sailing around the world, when you are preparing the boat, it includes preparing the crew as well. Knowledge and preparation will eliminate half of people's fears.

I remember hearing some of the Coast Guard guys telling me stories of how women couldn't even give their position in latitude and longitude to the Coast Guard, let alone turn the boat around to get to someone who had fallen overboard. In another story they told, they couldn't even communicate to the frantic woman because she was screaming on the VHF, but didn't let go of the button so that people could respond to her call. What a shame that her husband didn't take the time to make sure she knew what to do in an emergency and shame on that wife who didn't take the time or initiative to learn.

15. SHE HAS A FEAR ABOUT GOING INTO THE WATER OR CAN'T SWIM (13%)

I was not a great swimmer. I have told you the story about what my father did to me when I was a ten-year-old, and then having my so-called "friends" try and dunk me. It makes me angry when people are so disrespectful of someone who expresses a fear like this.

I do believe everyone should take some kind of minimal swimming lessons to make sure they could make it to shore or tread water until they are rescued. However, if you cannot swim, than it should be mandatory that you live in that life jacket at all times while on a boat, no exceptions.

Should we use this as a reason not to sail? I don't think so. Just take more precautions. Pay more attention to the weather and don't push your limits. Do what it takes to be safe and to feel safe. Just because you don't swim now, doesn't mean you can't learn even later in life. Don't let your fears hold you back. Use them to motivate you and to push yourself to new horizons. Fears can be overcome.

I found that learning to snorkel in the Bahamas changed everything for me in the water. The water was crystal clear and being able to breathe while propelling myself through the water with those big flippers made it fun. The sea life was spectacular to look at, and a new world opened up to me. I could see what was down under the water, so half of my fear was gone.

I will admit, though, that I still do not trust many people while I'm in the water. My advice for you, too, is don't trust everyone. Pick those few people who are on your side to help you and ignore the rest. Don't let people bully you or goad you. Do what works for you; if that means staying on the boat while others are in the water, you can always get a bucket and dump it over your head to wet yourself down and cool off.

I might also mention that cushions and swim noodles are great to have in the water if you are apprehensive. Do what makes you comfortable and if people don't respect your wishes, then they aren't your friends. Just avoid them, above all in the water.

16. SHE HATES TAKING TESTS (12%)

You do not have to get "certified" to take a good sailing class. Often people don't want to be put under the pressure of taking exams. I don't think it is necessary. You may decide down the road that it is important to you; however, the important thing is to gain knowledge, skills and confidence.

I'm not sure why this is such a common issue for women in classes, but I have my suspicions. I will make a few suggestions from comments I have received and personal observations.

There are a lot of women who have not been in a testing environment for a long time so this can be very stressful. When you have been out of school for ten, twenty or thirty years, a test can cause a lot of anxiety. Next, since a lot of women are learning to sail for the sake of their husbands, tests add stress to something that may not be that interesting for her in the first place. Another reason is that some women think a test might make them look stupid. They have already been sailing for a long time without really understanding what is going on. Lastly, some people just don't test well; a test may not be a good measure of their abilities.

Testing is a double-edged sword. On one side it can reveal that a woman is not knowledgeable enough, and then she will have to suffer embarrassment and humiliation in front of other people. On the flip side, testing can be confidence- building. She will now have proof of her knowledge, and will frequently be open to learning more since she now knows that she can learn this stuff.

Part of the problem is that women have been told for so long that something is wrong with them, because they could not grasp sailing the way the men were trying to teach them. We became convinced that there really must be something wrong with us, because everyone else is getting this except for us women. This is sad and frustrating because the fault does not lie with the student, but with the teacher. We all learn differently. Some people are auditory learners; they must hear it to understand the information. Others are kinesthetic, they learn by touch. The majority of women, and fifty-five percent of the entire population, including men, are visual learners. They need to see it in order to grasp it.

I read that people learn 400% more effectively when they learn things visually. Wow! Four hundred percent! So when you are being presented with information that is not coming across in the way you are wired to learn, it may be impossible for you to grasp the information.

Remember years ago before we understood about dyslexia? How many people thought they just couldn't learn, and now that we understand this learning disability, those same people can do and learn anything. They just have to learn by a different method than the average person. When people stopped telling them that they were stupid, and

gave them the tools to cope with their dyslexia, they could achieve at the level of their peers. My brother is a great example; he has dyslexia, and is a very accomplished and highly-regarded electrician.

Not all trainers in the sailing industry are created equal. In some organizations all a sailor has to do to become "certified to teach," is to prove their own sailing skills and that they are able to pass the test. That is not what it takes to be a good instructor. Teaching is an art and requires time on the trainer's part to learn and understand his students, especially adults. It also requires continuing his own training and preparing himself as well.

I have seen some men who are great at racing, but are Captain Bligh in the classroom, screaming and commanding those poor, clueless beginner students. Men have told me they don't want to be yelled at either. I think that is why some guys prefer to learn from women. They can ask what might seem like a dumb question and not be made to feel stupid.

Instructors are not monitored or given many opportunities for better-preparing themselves. And when there is a problem, there is often a double standard for male and female instructors. I would caution women to research your options for classes. When you sign up for a certification class, you do not know what kind of instructor you will be assigned. I don't know about you, but I'm not much of a gambler. Make sure you read Connie's story in the Gender Bias chapter. Her situation happened as I was getting this book to press. Find a school that supports their instructors and that will give you information specifically about your teacher ahead of time.

There is no reason why a woman cannot find a class that is either taught by a woman or a reputable man. If they teach part-time you can expect their teaching skills to be minimal. You can find a woman who follows the route to certification, if that is important to you, but there are many classes and seminars that women can take from women, in which you will get all the same information without the test and high cost. Don't let anyone tell you that you need to take a test to learn to sail; it's just not true.

Women also tend to teach instinctively, another way women need to learn. It was only through a lot of research that I found out why I teach the way I do. In talking with other instructors, I found I do not teach sailing the same way my male counterparts do.

Ladies, don't let the issue of testing stop you from learning or from becoming a confident sailor. Find the right environment, and you will find that you can do exceptionally well. I am confident that every woman out there can learn this stuff and be just as capable and confident as any guy...I have a list of women's resources at the end of the book and you can always go to the web site womensailing.com to find female captains, instructors and lots of women's programs and resources.

17. SHE THINKS GETTING THE BOAT READY IS TOO MUCH WORK (7%)

How hard is work when you love what you do? I can have my boat ready to sail in a matter of minutes and sails up in even less time. Part of making this time-consuming thing manageable is learning to develop a routine. There are also things like lazy jacks and roller furling systems that can add to the ease of sailing. "Too much work" is a statement that depends on how motivated you are to go sailing.

The typical routine for couples getting the boat ready to sail is: she goes down to the galley to make ready by securing items and stowing food and such, while he is on deck getting lines ready and making the boat ready to sail. Division of labor cuts the time in half. We do the same thing if we are going to pack the car to go on a picnic, or pack a suitcase to travel on vacation. My routine to get the boat ready doesn't take long at all now.

Most folks who live aboard accumulate too much junk on the boat and then it does take too much time and too much work. The live aboards end up never going sailing because of all that hassle.

The question is, do you know all the things to do to get the boat ready? It's all a matter of routine. You can go through the boat and make yourself a checklist. You'll find that once you understand it all, and

do it a few times, the time involved becomes less and less. There are some people who go overboard (not in the water) in planning, preparing and making the list and checking it twice, but isn't it a good thing to know you are prepared and safe?

18. SHE DOESN'T WANT TO DO THE HARD WORK ON THE BOAT(7%)

Sailing is not about the destination; it is about the journey. Getting the boat ready and sailing is about enjoying the whole process. I started out just trying to stay out of the way. I didn't know what to do so I felt like I was just in the way. It wasn't until I really started enjoying the whole thing that I decided I wanted to know more and do more. It's a process for us, one thing at a time and one step at a time. Start off doing what you want to do, and let someone else do the rest. It's what they enjoy doing anyway. Make agreements, I'll do this and you that. Soon it won't seem like work any more than the routine of showering and dressing in the morning.

People who don't want to work on the boat should not be expected to work. If you just want to go along for the ride, read a book and catch a few rays then that should be okay too. For those who want helm time, it means they get more because you don't want it anyway, and now it's a win-win situation.

Nobody should have to do anything that they don't want to, but if you are planning to go on a long voyage and not just day sailing you will eventually have to pitch in.

19. SHE DOESN'T HAVE THE TIME (4%)

This topic can be taken two ways. It may be that she is masking fear by saying she has no time, or it could be she needs to look at her priorities. Life for all of us gets busier and busier, but sometimes this is just an excuse for not taking a sailing class. Some people are worried about failure and others allow their fears to control them. You can make reasons or make results. Finding out the underlying reasons why we don't make time for something can help us overcome our excuse-making.

Learning to sail in the right environment is actually fun. It is also very rewarding to see how much you can learn and accomplish in a short period of time. We build on small successes. Taking small steps, like a seminar, is a good way to start the process. Once you see that it's not as difficult as you thought, you can then take the next step and continue to build those skills and abilities in a class or private setting.

We can always make time for those things that are important to us. When does it become important to you? When you are slipping off the dock lines and suddenly you realize that you are heading out now and you're really not ready? That's when real fear sets in, because it nags and stays at the forefront of your mind. Those *what ifs* are continuously clouding your thoughts so that you can't think of anything else.

Just a little preparation goes a long way. Would you leave without toilet paper? Shampoo? Food for the trip? How about water? Why is it that you are not at least as concerned about your preparation? You are at least as important as making sure the boat is stocked and prepared to take you to the next safe harbor. Think about it.

20. SHE IS TAKING THE CLASS FOR HIM, NOT HERSELF (3%)

Too often women will answer my question, "Why are you here?" With the response, "I'm doing it for him. It's his dream, not mine." She is in the sailing class reluctantly and is somewhat resistant to the process because of some or all of the things we have already discussed.

I would never have gotten into the sport of sailing had it not been for my boyfriend. He was the passion, not the boat. It was his dream to sail, his dream to buy the boat, his dream to live aboard and his dream to sail to Tahiti. However, I bought into that dream somewhere along the line. Suddenly his dream became my dream. Unfortunately, our relationship did not stand the test of time. Yet, here I sit with the course of my life forever changed because of that man's dream.

You will never do anything well unless you do it for yourself first.

Yes, men may inspire women. As I said, the entire course of my life changed as a result of this one man in my life and his passion. But I didn't really start growing until I made it my own. It has to be something you want, in order for you to embrace it fully. So set your mind on what it is that you would like to get out of it. Is it a concern for your own safety? Is it to know what to do in emergencies? Perhaps you would like to get to the point where you are comfortable as skipper? Only you know.

I know so many women that would never dream of taking their girlfriends out for a sail, because they don't know how to dock the boat. Wouldn't you like to know you can take your own boat out of the slip with or without your husband?

Fear is the reason so many people never live their lives to the fullest. Do you know what the word fear stands for? False Evidence that Appears Real.

So many of the issues that we have just discussed can be overcome by learning and understanding the wind and how to sail your boat. Knowledge removes many of our fears. And sometimes we need to understand and accept that there is an element of fear in doing anything new. Just don't let that hold you back from doing whatever it is that you want to do.

I have traveled single-handed on my boat throughout the Bahamas. I have also traveled from Copenhagen to Greece and throughout Europe alone. Was I afraid? Very often I was – but it didn't stop me. I would sometimes question myself and ask what the heck I was doing, but I would just keep going. And the best part of it is that I can say, "I did it!" I live up to being a Tididi, because I do it even though most of the time it is backwards. So you can be a Tididi too.

My life is completely changed forever, because of the dream Jack had. I am on this path because of Jack. However, now it's mine. What I do and what I have accomplished is because of what I chose after we parted company. I could have turned away from the whole sailing life, but I chose this instead.

So we can, in the end, come up with reasons or results, excuses or accomplishments. We can run from life or have fun running the race of life. Do you want to grow old and have regrets when you look back on your life, or have stories to tell the grandchildren? Do you want to enjoy the trip on the boat, or live in fear of what might happen? Aren't you worth the time, effort and even the expense of it? What is your peace of mind worth? The reality is that half of the things we fear will never happen, and preparing ourselves can prevent the other half. If you don't want to go through life with fear or regret, do something about it.

Remember the foundation of sailing is about understanding the invisible wind. When you get a hold of this, and then learn the thought process, there isn't anything on a boat that you can't do just as well as your mate. No house stands firm without a good foundation.

FIVE

GENDER BIAS IN BOATING

When women step into roles that are traditionally male-dominated, they endure a lot of ill treatment from their male competitors.

A TIME FOR CHANGE

Although most people don't want to acknowledge or discuss this issue, it is a necessary part of bringing awareness and change to the sailing community. I realize this may be a sensitive issue for some. I am in no way trying to put down the whole male gender, but there are some men who need to be put in their place. I know I am not going to win any popularity contests here, however, I believe it will only be those people who truly look down on women that will not take what I'm saying in the helpful spirit in which it is given. So if you take offense, I suspect you may be one of the offenders! But those who really care about their female sailing partners or female students will be able to hear a new perspective and effect change, making sailing, and boating in general, more welcoming to women.

The comments shared here are often things that have been told to me by men about men. Unfortunately, there are still many "old school" men in the sailing community who feel that women are, at best, an intrusion, and at worst, inferior and incompetent. It is shocking to find in today's more-tolerant society, where minorities have gained respect, a community where treating women differently is still considered acceptable. I find a lot of what is being said hurtful and offensive as discrimination always is. We need to stop ignoring the elephant in the room and say "enough is enough" with the way women are still being treated in the sailing industry. Let me make it clear up front that I'm not saying that this is happening all the time or everywhere. But it is happening often enough that something must be done about it.

It wasn't that long ago that women were considered bad luck on a boat. I cannot tell you for certain why that was, but I think it probably had something to do with them distracting men from their duties. When women were first allowed to sail on Coast Guard ships, my father was outraged. When I heard about what it was like on the ships, I could understand where he was coming from. Firstly, women were given special treatment: they had their own private quarters and bathrooms, and, of course, they didn't have to shave their heads! Some of guys felt resentful. Secondly, when the women were not physically able to keep up with the men, the guys would have to pick up the slack. Lastly, some guys were getting distracted and began thinking with the wrong head!

A debacle happened on one of the ships on which my father sailed. The military does not allow married people to serve on the same ship for good reason. The result of a secret marriage and a jealous husband was another guy ending up dead. What an unnecessary incident! It never would have happened if women had not been allowed onboard. It's easy to see my father's point of view: If women want to play in a man's world, then they should not expect to be treated differently. But remember, he was coming from a military setting. In pleasure-boating and cruising, when we are among friends, we shouldn't expect to see such a militant viewpoint!

To the men who respect and encourage women, I applaud and thank you. We need more men to stand up for women in this industry. It is my belief that the more we understand our differences, the more tolerance we will exhibit toward each other. My goal is to see more appreciation for those differences and more support for women on the water.

Unfortunately, every year I have at least one guy aboard my boat who will challenge me, argue with me and make a scene. I didn't realize

what was happening at first, but it I do know it is a testosterone thing, but I will tell you that my tolerance level is very low for that type of behavior! There is no place for disrespect for anyone in the position of leadership on a boat, especially for a professional captain, and in a learning atmosphere, to boot.

The more I understand gender differences, the more I believe that men who feel they need to challenge women have a problem with their own masculinity and use bravado to hide their insecurity. Women usually don't fight for top dog position. Women are generally the peacemakers and want a level playing field, as you will see when we examine gender differences. I can't stress enough that aggressive and childish behavior is absolutely unacceptable under any circumstance, but especially when on someone else's boat or in a classroom setting. If you are crew, and observe an abusive pattern, should you have an opportunity to leave the situation, I recommend that you do so. And don't be afraid to report it. Remember, three similar incidences constitute a pattern and people rarely change. Can you live with this behavior long-term? If you can't, I suggest that you run in the other direction.

There are those who either do not understand or who are unwilling to examine evidence that might change their viewpoints to accept that the genders are very different. I have heard, even read in some articles, men claiming that these differences don't exist. I can tell you that ignorance may be bliss but science proves differently. Usually, it is the older generation and that old-school masculine type who would rather deny than adapt or admit they have been wrong-headed. For too long women have been treated as if they are either stupid or incapable, because they are unable to grasp the same information in the same way or at the same pace as their male counterparts.

It is true that women may start out learning more slowly, especially when they are being asked to do it in a manner that is not natural to their way of processing. However, women are more than capable of not only learning, but like Ellen MacArthur, who single-handed her boat around the world, excelling at whatever it is that they put their minds to.

Discrimination toward women in the sailing industry is still very widespread. Until both men and women in this industry take a stand

and speak out, this type of behavior will continue.

Allow me to share my own experience with gender bias. When I was taking the course to become an instructor, I was assigned to a Captain Bligh, who clearly did not like women. I felt like quitting every day because this man would continually criticize me and change his expectations. When asked to teach a skill like tacking, I would go through the process and he would then say, "That is not what I wanted." However, he never conveyed what he did want, so I couldn't win. By day three of the five-day qualification process everyone in the group acknowledged that this Instructor Qualifier was treating me differently. With the help of two large male classmates who came to my defense, I decided to stay and finish the program.

By the last day I'd had enough of this guy and when he started yelling at me (for the last time) I finally turned around to him, pulled my hands off the wheel and said, "I'm done. You take the helm." He backed off after that, but I thought for sure he would fail me (he didn't). I hate to tell you that this man is still teaching in southeast Florida. A fellow instructor told me that when women step on his boat he tells them, "I will tell it to you once and if you don't get it, it's not my problem." What a #*@$%&!. The school and organization he represents allow him to get away with it. They refuse to even confront instructors like him and instead try to put the blame on female students, brushing them off as if they are just whiners or busybodies.

I submit that this man is a jerk and should not be allowed to teach, but when you are among what is still the "good ol' boys club, "guess who gets shut out? I'm sorry to say that this organization refused to even look into the matter, and this has been the pattern of this organization. So is it any wonder women don't want to be in that kind of environment? And isn't it funny how people who discriminate tend to take the greatest offense when they are called on it? They behave defensively rather than apologize for their actions. Well, maybe it is more sad than funny.

Women are not very willing to come forward for fear of retribution or dismissal. With regard to my Captain Bligh, I did try to report the problem, but the organization chose to ignore it. I was told that if I pursued it I would be black-listed. So women like me have chosen to

keep quiet in order to pursue a career we love. The woman whose story you will read in a moment said she wasn't willing to approach the owner of the sailing school where she trained, because, in her own words, *"my life is complicated enough, and one needs to pick one's battles."* She is no coward, but asked me to present her comments anonymously. For some reason, women continue to suffer in silence. And everyone ignores the elephant in the room.

Over the last few years I've been collecting stories from Baby Boomers that grew up before the Women's Lib movement, and from young women on college and university sailing teams. The number of so-called professionals in this industry that still discriminate is surprising. To avoid a lawsuit, I will not name the worst culprits, but you would be appalled to learn that the offending organization is a large, well-established and widely-recognized sailing school. Perhaps because they are so large and well-known, they still get away with it.

When women step into roles that are traditionally male-dominated, they endure a lot of ill treatment from their male competitors. I don't fully understand why, but it seems that these men feel threatened. I can tell you I have experienced a lot of it myself.

The more stories I hear, the more upset I get. If a woman steps forward to report or resolve an unpleasant situation, the guilty party will do everything he can to discredit and slander the woman, sometimes with the aid of the organization to which he belongs. A good example from recent current events is Sarah Palin. There was a derogatory article published about her that was negative and hurtful and contained very little truth. The press finally attacked her and her family so much that she stepped out of the ring. Here is a confident, successful woman who is handling both her career and family. Is she perfect? I doubt it. But I don't see the same kind of attack being waged on men.

There is something wrong with this picture: why is hostility toward a female instructor tolerated? Just because someone paid for a class does not mean he should be allowed to behave inappropriately. All instructors, male and female alike, should be able to stand up to and protect themselves from abusive students. Too many people in positions of authority in the industry are still willing to turn their backs on the problem, and displace blame when confronted. They make excuses because they are not willing to take responsibility. A woman with a legitimate complaint is not just "P.M.S.-ing" or being a "b****," contrary to popular accusation. I hope that this upsets you enough to call these people to task if given the opportunity.

To offer another personal example, I once had a male captain spread a rumor that I was irresponsible. I had only met this guy once or twice, so it wasn't like we even knew each other. When I learned about his comments, I called and confronted him. He told me that he heard that I had taken off and sailed to Tahiti. I said, "So what?" He told me, "Well you were scheduled to teach a class." I responded, "Not that it's any of your business, but the office was given ample time to replace me." Then I asked him, "What is the difference between me doing a delivery and you doing a delivery?" He started back-stepping and stuttering, then replied, "Oh, I didn't know you were getting paid for it." It shut him up but do you think he apologized for telling lies about me?

I can tell you that I personally know a lot of women who are currently enduring this kind of treatment in silence. It is time for the men and women in the sailing industry who agree that this is wrong to speak up! Let the offenders know that this is not acceptable! I don't care who you are!

❧

The correspondence you are about to read came to me the summer of 2009, while I was writing this book. This all-too-common story exemplifies what needs to change about sailing organizations and boating in general to make it more welcoming to women. Ladies, the good news is you don't have to tolerate bad behavior from this type of male instructor—there is a growing number of female captains to choose from if you want to take lessons.

It is to prevent you from ending up with an instructor like the one below that I encourage women to do more research and "know before you go." First, a bit of background information: Connie and George spent about a week training with me before she and her husband took an advanced class elsewhere. This is an email forwarded to me from Connie, verbatim:

Our coastal cruising class was a joke. The instructor was nice enough, but didn't really teach anything structured - just a few pointers here and there throughout the day. He gave us the exams at the start of class and told us to have them done by the end, and then gave us the key so we corrected them ourselves. At least George and I researched the answers - I think our classmate just copied off the answer key! Additionally, our instructor was at an ebb of personal enthusiasm about sailing; he was about to trade his boat in for a power boat, and sadly, he seemed more interested in getting a beer at the end of the day than in teaching.

We did one anchoring and one mooring exercise, and he showed our classmate and George how to use the outboard, but I was never shown. It felt like that with a lot of lessons - he'd just start teaching the guys and I would either have been relegated to some other activity or just left to scramble over at the last minute after he'd already started.

I didn't get any navigation training. To be fair, George and the classmate had both already had navigation (George studied it on his own and took the test at a local library) so they would have been bored. Our instructor never once sat down and did ANY kind of formal instructional session that would have given him time to talk about navigation.

The class was supposed to take us from Mystic CT to Block Island, and then to Newport, then back to Mystic. I'm not sure how legitimately poor the weather was in Block Island Sound during our class, but we ended up doing a much shorter sail around Long Island Sound. The whole time I was being delegated to do the less critical tasks, with the 2 male students taking over the more important stuff. I was thinking, "This would be a much better experience with Captain Josie!"

Captain Josie is a truly gifted instructor. Most sailing

instructors know how to sail; few of them actually know how to teach. She appreciates different learning styles and teaches accordingly with an array of learning aids that she has developed herself. Each day of class was a series of well-structured, highly focused lessons that brought us quickly from nervous beginners to being confident that we could sail. As a couple, we both appreciated her emphasis on communication and teamwork. When ever has such an intense learning experience been so much fun?

CB

The following is a list sums up the problems, which push women out of sailing—either teaching or taking classes. There are many examples of bias, myth and misunderstanding that I have heard or experienced first-hand. Please help me stop this gender injustice. This has no place in the sailing community anymore.

There are some men who are just oblivious to their partner's fears and issues. These guys will write her anxiety off as invalid or inconsequential if they don't personally feel the same thing or understand where she's coming from. She is accused of imagining things, over-reacting, freaking out or acting crazy. Too often women's fears are dismissed as being stupid or unfounded. While one person may not feel the same thing, it doesn't mean that it is not real for the other person. We all handle problems, fears and stress in different ways. Avoiding or ignoring problems does not make them go away. In fact, it can cause small problems to become big problems—big enough to make a woman leave the boat temporarily, or worse, leave her sailing partner permanently. Men have fears but express or deal with them in a different way than women do.

I just recently heard about an instructor who told the student-husband that he thinks the best way to teach a woman is the "sink-or-swim" method. This instructor thinks that more people should use scare tactics to force women to "deal with it ." He really believes this will work! How insensitive and ignorant can one guy be? I pity the woman who ends up in a sailing class with a guy like this for an instructor. This type of person gives sailing a bad name. (To be perfectly honest, I'd like to see someone punch this guy in the nose!) If you want to send a woman packing, go ahead and scare her to death. Terrorizing someone, especially a beginner, either male or female, will not motivate him any more than yelling at or belittling him.

There are a lot of instructors out there who may be good sailors but not good teachers. Some instructors demand perfection and often end up yelling and screaming at students who really don't know what is expected of them. The truth remains that the responsibility for student achievement and satisfaction rests on the shoulders of the instructor, and, ultimately, the sailing school operators. Unless a student is just uncooperative and unwilling to learn, the onus is on the instructor, who must be prepared and personable. When students do well, it is a direct reflection of the instructors' ability to convey information well.

For example, a "racer" mentality is a detriment to the learning process, especially for beginners (though not all racers are bad instructors). I know there are instructors who push their boats to the limit. They will be heeled over because they think it's fun, not having any consideration for new students who may be uncomfortable or feel as if the boat is out of control. Nervous students are unlikely to learn anything new while their focus is on what they will do if they fall in the water or the boat capsizes.

Some men don't feel masculine unless they put women in a passive role. There are insecure teachers who will not even teach a woman, or a husband and wife team. They fear teaching a woman will mean losing their position of dominance. They may have a point—if she learned that she was strong and capable she may not continue to allow their abusive behavior! Knowledge is power and when you know what you are doing, people cannot bully you or push you around as easily. A bully is simply someone who feels insecure about either who they are, or what they know (or, rather, don't know) and makes up for it by being more aggressive.

We will probably never completely eliminate the chauvinistic worldview; some men will always feel that women are inferior. But we can exert some positive peer pressure and start speaking up and saying that despite their views, their actions will not be tolerated. To the good guys: Please take a stand for your woman, whether she is your wife or girlfriend, sister, or co-worker. Don't ignore sexist jokes and comments, because you can help make them unacceptable.

A last and somewhat uncomfortable topic, but one which I cannot ignore, is sexual harassment. Women still endure teasing and sexual innuendos in, on and around boats. They should not have to endure unwanted advances. I was fortunate to sail in Greece with a guy who understood the problems women endure in the boating community. He was originally looking for crew to help him take the boat from the Bahamas to the Mediterranean. While he was showing me the boat, he looked me in the eye and told me in a straight-forward manner, "Don't worry, sex is not a part of the job." Was I ever relieved that he understood my concern before I ever had to speak it!

This guy was the envy of every anchorage. Because they feel safe with him, he always had a boatload of women. I was one of an all-female crew. Every place we went we were asked, "What's he got that I haven't got?" And we would just smile and tell them that he was a great guy. And it was true.

Some say the best way to deal with gender problems is to just not bring the gender problems aboard. I agree if it means peace-keeping and treating everyone, male or female, with respect. But if they're saying that women are not welcome, or are somehow supposed to quit being women once they step aboard a boat, I take exception. Listen, I wear lipstick when I sail because it protects my lips from sunburn and makes me feel feminine. Does that affect my ability to sail? I do not think that women should have to compromise their femininity to be equal partners with men on a boat. Some men perceive a woman as weak if she is feminine. But if she doesn't wear lipstick, so to speak, or is seen as trying to be like a man, she's also given a hard time.

There must be a happy medium between the extremes of "butch" and "bi&*^ch" where a woman can respect and be respected by men on boats in professional and personal settings. Women shouldn't even be categorized with words like these, but I hear them all the time! Until we bring this into the light, exposing it for what it is, and refuse to accept it, women sailors and instructors will continue to endure discrimination.

I could tell many more stories about students who were disappointed by their introduction to sailing because they took lessons from someone who either scared them, disrespected them or completely ignored their needs. I could go on and on about female instructors who were yelled at, threatened and man-handled by male students, and were reprimanded for flunking said aggressors. But I think you get my point. If this industry is going to be sustained and expanded, women need to know they are in a safe environment.

I've said it before, but I'll say it again: if you are a woman or a couple looking for classes, do your homework! Women are relational and need to find an instructor that will tailor his or her instruction to meet a woman's needs. My advice is to find out everything you can about an instructor before you commit to a class. I would even suggest that if you cannot learn about the instructor's credentials or get a reference prior to the class, that you find another place to go.

The Women's Sailing Connection is all about helping women find female instructors and schools that support couples. You can search for a woman captain or instructor by location or captain's name. You can read about her background and experience and even speak with her prior to taking the class. For more information, see the last chapter, *Women's Resources.*

Now that you've heard the bad news, here is the good: There are many men in the industry that are great teachers, friends and supporters. If it hadn't been for the men in the industry that have been supportive and helpful to me, I would have probably left the sailing community a long time ago. They have encouraged and cheered me up when I have been hurt by lies, personal attacks, or aggression from rude male colleagues. And to the husbands and boyfriends who get this, thank you for being there for your female companion! A man gets to realize his dreams when the woman in his life is happy on the boat.

TWO ON A BOAT HOW TO KEEP IT AFLOAT

Six

Gender Differences

She exclaimed,"What do you mean, the seacock broke off in your hand?! Are we sinking?!" He calmly replied, "It's okay...I had a wooden plug! The bilge pump will take care of the rest. Don't worry about it."

HIS & HER WAY TO LEARN, PROCESS & COMMUNICATE

While some people may try to put me in a box labeled "stereotype" I assure you I don't fit into any box very well. I am neither defending nor do I fit a traditional gender role. The information I am sharing comes from many years of research by a variety of experts on the subject. Researchers have spent years observing people of all ages. Know that I am not just conveying my own opinions here, and have tried to remain objective.

Our perspective in life can be affected by our past, by traditions, by social economics, by family and by genetics. All these things play a role in who we become. Gender identity is only one aspect of our personalities, but a powerful one. We all have certain hormones that affect our feminine and masculine tendencies. (Some have more than others.) Some behavior is learned and some is from our environment. For example, while I may be one hundred percent female, and I like being that way, I did become the chief breadwinner when it came to raising my son as a single mom. I think that predisposed me to take on a lot more of the traditionally masculine roles and become more independent as a result.

I fell immediately into what would be considered the traditional female role on the boat when I first learned to sail. But now, as the captain and person in charge while teaching classes, I exhibit more masculine inclinations when I am on the boat. This gets me into trouble from time to time because some men want to challenge me. So you won't see any stereotyping from me; that's not what this is about.

We all have masculine and feminine tendencies. I think that a well-balanced person has a combination of both genders' characteristics though they usually lean more heavily in one direction or the other. And some people fit a traditional gender role one hundred percent. But too extreme in either direction causes problems.

I'm sure you know some men who are just men's men. They are masculine in every sense of the word. I have a few friends who are like that and if we spend too much time together we start butting heads, because he just cannot understand the female perspective at all. So it comes across to me as extreme insensitivity. He is set in his ways and there isn't anybody or anything that is going to change his views and perceptions. Do you know anybody like that?

On the flip side, there are some women who will not even risk breaking a fingernail. She will wear the wrong kind of shoes (for looks rather than comfort) and heaven forbid it if you should mess up her hair or makeup. She changes her mind and cries when she feels like it. She is the typical high-maintenance female . Do you know someone like that?

And sometimes we reverse roles completely. My boyfriend loved to cook. I can cook, but I would rather have someone cook for me. It used to be said that the way to a man's heart was through his stomach, but I say it's just the opposite now. Guys can woo a woman by cooking for her. If he is good at it, he may even win her. I like that role reversal.

We all have some traits from each side. We can move between typical gender responses, and have one or the other dominate for a time or a situation. Sailing is about being flexible. Have you ever heard the saying that things that don't bend, break? We need to be ready to

change course when there is an obstacle or to stay in the anchorage one more day to wait for the weather window to open. Being on the sea means that you are not necessarily in control. If you try to oppose Mother Nature, she will always win. The same is true in relationships. We must be ready to accept the masculine and feminine parts of our mates and ourselves without pigeonholing, and be willing to take on tasks that may not fit traditional expectations, while still accepting that our partner may have uniquely masculine or feminine traits and perspectives.

I think that the man who is willing to read this book and take to heart the needs of the woman in his life is a special breed. A woman can feel confident to put her life in the hands of this kind of man, because he really cares about others and not just about himself. So guys, I hope you will open up your minds and see what you can glean from the information in this book, as it is meant in the most positive way.

We will look at gender differences and discuss them one by one. Keep in mind that although I am coming from the female perspective, the information that I share regarding men comes directly from insights men have shared with me. I may be an expert at being a woman, but I want to give a balanced approach. The goal is not to stereotype, over-generalize, or offend, but to offer insight and understanding. I hope that you learn to be more open-minded towards your mate's differences. If you stop trying to change your partner to be more like you and instead embrace the differences, you will appreciate each other more as a result. So, listen up ladies *and* gentlemen!

HIS PERSPECTIVE versus HER PERSPECTIVE

Allow me some creative leeway here. Remember the movie, *Pirates of the Caribbean*? That is how men imagine the cruising lifestyle. He sees going cruising as a doorway to adventure and freedom. He is enticed by the excitement of stepping out into the unknown. He likes to fantasize about pirates and wenches, danger and mystery and the possibility of treasure. Men need to test the limits, conquer something, and leave a mark on the world .

I was recently at a Latitudes & Attitudes party in the Pacific

Northwest. I couldn't believe how these guys got into the whole pirate thing. It wasn't just about dressing up—they were really getting into pretending to be wild, carefree, and unrestrained. Everyone was well-behaved, but they where having a blast pretending to be on the loose. They dressed to the nines with hats,  swords and eye patches. Many of them had wigs with long dreadlocks and the word "*Aaargh*" seemed to be the only word they knew.

Now think of a movie that would depict the way women see going cruising. It would have to be *The Perfect Storm*. Imagine that small boat attempting to climb, like an ant, up that hundred-foot wave, only to be engulfed and swallowed up by the ocean, never to be heard from again. She is terrified of the prospect in stepping out into that unknown territory.

 Typically, the woman in a relationship is the nurturer and caretaker. She wants to protect and to be protected. She does not want to be forced in to an ordeal that could take her life. She needs safety, comfort, and a dry and stable environment. Her greatest concern is security. She doesn't want to tempt the elements. What ever you do, all she asks is, "Just don't kill us!" And she means both of you, since she is just as worried about something happening to her mate as to herself. If she doesn't know how to get back without you, your loss translates into her death, too.

The dread of running into that hundred-foot rogue wave put me into my own private panic. So I left land with an undercurrent of fear, believing that I was heading out to my death rather than an adventure of a lifetime. Of course, if she is already a sailor; a woman knows the truth about cruising. Ninety-five percent of the time it is calm, peaceful and serene. It is a get-away from the everyday routines and responsibilities of a land-life. And the fear of catastrophe usually does not dominate her thinking.

These two pictures depict life on the ocean. One is the ninety-five percent calm, warm and peaceful downwind run. The other is the five percent wild and windy or wet passage when the squalls kick up. I experienced both on my voyage to the South Pacific. Of the twenty-five days we were at sea, we had only a couple of stormy days. But that slim five-percent stormy picture will keep most women from ever experiencing the other wonderful ninety-five percent. These pictures are analogous of men and women, too. Guess whose desires are like a storm at sea, and whose like the calm ocean swells of a sunny day?

Men are the explorers, the adventurers, the trailblazers and the daredevils. They love the excitement and the prospect of danger more than women can fathom. If it wasn't for men, America would never have been discovered. I believe that men do get scared sometimes, but they are not as willing to show it, or it surfaces in a different way.

Women, on the other hand, need security and safety. Some women will go to the ends of the earth with their husbands, as long as they know that they will survive the ordeal. Some will go reluctantly and with trepidation. Then there are others, like my mother, who never allow their husbands to get them out there in the first place. My father had his adventures, but not with her by his side.

Since cave-man days, the men were the hunters, risking life and limb, chasing the wild beast to bring home the meat. The women stayed back and were the gatherers and the child bearers. It is much safer to pull the fruit off the trees and pick the vegetables out of the garden. Before you get upset and say that women can do the same things as men, understand that I'm not saying otherwise, rather that we have for millennia taken on certain roles, and even our body designs dictate physical capabilities.

Women are typically not as physically as strong as men. Does that mean we cannot do the same things? No. It means that we sometimes have to find a different way of approaching the same tasks. Women have learned how to work smarter instead of harder. They use leverage instead of muscle. On a boat, there are all sorts of new technologies that make the work of sailing easy for anyone. An electric winch can hoist the main at the touch of a button. And men don't feel any less capable using the electric winch (just less tired).

I had juvenile rheumatoid arthritis, so I do not have a lot of strength in my hands. This affects my ability to do some of the jobs on the boat. I do try and I like to know I can do things by myself but very often I have to ask for help because I just physically cannot do the job. I do not feel that it makes me any less of a person, captain, instructor or woman. It is what it is, and because I know my limitations, I will ask for help when I need it, or compensate in some other way.

Let's look at some of the major differences between men and women in the ways they learn, process and communicate. Once you gain a basic understanding of these contrasts, it will be easy to make slight changes in the way you talk to each other, so that you can make sure that you are understood, and are working together to meet each others' needs. Ideally, the two views will balance each other out. I did not put this list in any particular order, but you will see that a lot of the characteristics overlap and interrelate.

FEMININE vs. MASCULINE
1. Relationship-oriented vs. Results-oriented
2. Needs Security vs. Needs Challenges
3. Relational & Visual vs. Linear & Logical
4. Verbal vs. Non-verbal
5. Team-Oriented vs. Chain of Command
6. Needs a Game Plan vs. Plays it as it Comes
7. Wants to Know Why vs. Wants to Know How
8. Non-responsive in Crisis vs. Try-Anything Approach
9. Overreacts vs. Under-reacts
10. Caretaker & Supporter vs. Protector & Provider
11. Emotional Decision-making vs. Logical Decision-making
12. Blames internally vs. Blames externally
13. Needs time to Make Decisions vs. Makes Decisions Quickly
14. Multi-tasks vs. Mono-Tasks

1. SHE IS RELATIONSHIP-ORIENTED, HE IS RESULTS-ORIENTED.

She says, "How does leaving affect me and my environment?" He says, "How can I get to...the Bahamas, the Caribbean, Tahiti, etc.?" She bases her decisions on things that affect her environment, personal safety, and comfort. And if there are children in the picture, she is a determined mother hen protecting her chicks. She needs to see how the consequences will relate to her personally and those for whom she cares. His need is to see how things interrelate to achieve a purpose. For him it is taking steps to buy the boat or finally take off to go cruising.

When teaching women, I know she needs to know what is going to happen to her personally before she ever leaves the dock. She needs to know how it will affect her life, her safety, and her environment. She questions safety first. If she understands how the situation will affect her, and that she will be okay, then, and only then, can she focus on the boat and learning the aspects of sailing. By teaching her how to feel the wind instead of where it is on the boat, she will have a greater understanding of how it will affect her own personal environment.

Most of the women who have sailed with me, told me that they read a sailing book but never got much out of it. This caused them to come to the class with a lot of reservations. They were convinced before they ever stepped on the boat that they could not learn the information. The next most common thing I hear is, "I need to do it to learn it." It stands to reason that since the majority of women are visual learners, they need that hands-on training to see how everything is interrelated and how it will affect what is happening around them.

By using the *Sailing Wind Wheel* tool, I have had almost every woman (and of course the men, too) grasping an understanding of the wind the first time out on the water. They can conceptualize where the wind is in relationship to them personally and how it will affect the boat. They also gain a quicker ability to determine the right way to turn the boat—they understand, not just memorize the points of sail. It's absolute magic for them. Since so much of sailing is about understanding the wind, I can see how so many women always feel disconnected from what is going on, and consequently they do not feel safe. This relates to our next gender difference.

2. SHE NEEDS SECURITY, HE NEEDS CHALLENGES.

She asks, "Am I going to die if I do this?" I know some people laugh, but whether it is on a conscious or subconscious level, women need to have their safety and security issues dealt with first. When people get this, something like taking a sailing class is going to be viewed differently. In the class itself, the trainer and the spouse need to address her concerns. And women need to realize that with knowledge fear diminishes.

I had one female student early in my career who repeatedly said, "And then we die?" I would explain something and she would finish it with, "And then we die?" She and her husband had bought a thirty-four boat and she couldn't enjoy it because she was sure she would die. To demonstrate that she would not die, I told her to just let go of the helm. Of course, she was too paralyzed with fear to realize the dynamics of the boat. So I took the helm, let go of the wheel; the boat rounded up into the wind, the sails luffed and the boat stopped. Once she caught on that she wasn't going to die, she had a blast from then on out.

When Didier and I were saying goodbye to my family at Thanksgiving to go to the Bahamas, in my mind it wasn't "goodbye, see you soon," it was "goodbye, you will never see me again because I'm sure I'm going to die in a rogue wave." I really believed that we would be taken by surprise and the boat would capsize and we would never be heard from again. Even though I knew we had done everything possible to insure that the boat was seaworthy, like having her hauled out and checked inside and out, having the bottom painted and through-hulls replaced, and so forth and so on, it was the fear of the unknown possibilities that caused that knot in the pit of my stomach that just wouldn't go away. I think on a conscious level I knew it was bit irrational, but I couldn't shake that fear of all the *what-ifs*.

I really had mixed emotions; I was finally accomplishing my dream of going cruising on my own boat, a prospect which had kept me motivated for years, yet now that I was on the verge of accomplishing this monumental goal, I was scared half to death. I felt like a little kid going to Disney Land for the first time and standing in line for Space Mountain !

There have been many times when I have had female students experience anxiety about what we were doing and feel overwhelmed. I don't believe that scaring them more is going to shake it out of them. If a woman feels afraid or overwhelmed, it usually comes to the surface in the form of tears. For men, it surfaces as anger.

I reassured one woman by saying, "Here is the deal, when I panic you can panic. Until then you don't need to panic." It was what she needed to hear. Another woman was so nervous that when I said we were going to do donuts under power, she crouched down in the cockpit. I let her stay there where she felt safe until she could see that it would be okay. Trust has to be earned; it is not just given. Some people just need extra reassurance that things are not as bad as they think. The worst thing to do is dismiss or ignore fear.

When you keep in mind that women need safety first you can take the necessary little steps to comfort and reassure them. Allow them time to adjust, and build trust and confidence little by little.

A man, on the other hand, will dive head-on into new environments, even if he doesn't know the outcome. He is willing to push the limits more aggressively. How far will this boat heel? How fast will the boat go? How strong of a wind can this boat handle? These are the questions that captivate a man but make his female first-mate cringe! She wants to see that the boat stays under control and its passengers safe, returning to the dock with minimal risk of injury or loss of life. She wants to be comfortable and know she isn't going to have to do an M.O.B. drill.

She may be willing to let him push the limits, if he is willing to stop when she says "enough." That is when guys can show her that her needs are being met, just by taking the reef or easing the main sheet a little bit. Showing her that he understands her needs goes a long way to getting her to trust him. And she may then be willing to go to the next level with him, even though it may seem risky, because she knows he won't kill her.

Another example is that she would rather be at the anchorage at a decent hour, preferably in the afternoon so they can get the boat settled in while there is still daylight. Then they have time to do a little exploring and have a nice dinner before sunset. But he would say, "Let's try and push further and get to the next island today. It's not much further, but we may not make it until dark." This will seem fine to him, but put her under stress. Now they are trying to make their way into an unknown anchorage in the dark, without any land references and they can hear the water crashing on the rocks nearby. To one it is a challenge, to the other a disaster waiting to happen!

That is exactly how it felt to me when we arrived in Nuka Hiva at four o'clock in the morning. It was pitch black. We were using as guides five lights that the captains said were in the guidebook. We had a night scope, so I could try to see where the land was; I knew it was there because I could hear the waves crashing. We were closer to land than makes me comfortable. We couldn't see anything except the lights until we got in closer, and with the help of the night scope, some rocks.

It turned out that the lights we thought were on land were actually the lights on the spreaders of a one hundred fifty foot sailing yacht. They had deck lights at the level of each of the five spreaders. It was unbelievable—we were on a collision course with an anchored boat, thinking it was the lit entrance to the channel! That was too stressful for me. If I had been the captain, I would have learned about the entrance to the harbor, read everything I could about the area, ignored the advice of others, and I definitely would not have made the landing until daylight. But then again, I'm a girl. The truth is that we made it in there okay. And with the experience I have now, I don't see what they did as being too risky. A man will get the adventure going, but a woman will help everyone on the boat stay safe on the way. It's all about finding balance.

3. HER MODE OF LEARNING IS RELATIONAL AND VISUAL vs. HIS IS LINEAR AND LOGICAL.

When there are two people who learn differently, one may appear

to grasp the information more quickly. Although it appears that one is stronger, the other may simply need the material presented in a different way. It is the job of a teacher to give the "weaker" student more information and time to process. This is true for women learning sailing. Women have struggled for a long time with learning to sail because the information has always been presented in a way that makes sense to men. It is not impossible for her to learn, but it takes longer when she is not taught the way she is wired to learn.

For example, every visual aid for presenting the points of sail in all the beginner sailing books, is presented in the way men learn. The diagrams used can be difficult to begin with because the pictures are two-dimensional, while sailing is three-dimensional. Since women don't generally learn in a linear fashion, the methods used by these books have been the biggest obstacle for women in becoming proficient in this sport. The pictures in sailing books also show how the wind affects the boat, but women learn by how it affects them.

When someone does not understand new information in the manner in which it is presented, whether it is terminology or skill practice, it is important to give him more ways than one to help him master the subject at hand. The problem will not be resolved by repeating the same thing over and over again and in the same way. If someone doesn't grasp it the first time, the teacher needs to find another way to convey the information. In a classroom setting, this may mean that others in the class may have to hear what they already know in order to allow everyone get on the same page. There are as many ways of teaching as there are modes of learning. A good teacher will use lots of tools to convey new information: he can demonstrate it, write it, draw diagrams, use models or other visual aids and so on.

If a sailing instructor is willing to teach women the way they are wired to learn, they will excel. Firstly, because women tend to be verbal processors, they will generally need more time to talk about the new information. They actually think out loud. I know it drives men crazy. I will address that later when I talk about communication.

Secondly, women are relational and visual learners. She needs to learn about all the parts and how they relate to the whole, and to visualize what it will be like. When she has "seen" it and knows she is going to be safe, she will be willing to go to the next step. Guys, on the other hand, will say, "Lets just get this boat out of the slip and go sailing. We will learn as we go." And that is what they will do. A guy instructor will start pointing out the parts of the boat as they are getting it ready and once out there sailing the instructor will explain what to do step by step, in a linear fashion, as they are actually doing it. If you want to give a woman an anxiety attack, that method is sure to do it for some.

A woman asks, what does it look and feel like before I try it? When women learn something new, they need the overall picture first. The worst thing you can do when teaching a woman to sail is to give her a task like 'sheeting in' and say, "Just do this when I tell you." Without the full disclosure of the whole process, she may worry that if she does it wrong something bad will happen. Unless she understands her task completely, a woman becomes fearful that what she is doing will adversely affect the boat, or worse, hurt someone. It will make it easier for a woman to try a new experience if she can see the end result and not be as afraid of making mistakes.

In one of my all-women's classes, each woman had a different job to do on the boat. One was releasing the jib sheet and the other sheeting in when we tacked. One woman just would not let go of her sheet, no matter what I said. She released it, but kept the line in her hand. After we got the sail trimmed I asked her why she was not letting go of the line. She said, "I thought we would lose control of the sail if I completely let go." So I had my own lesson to learn! Instructors should always be learning and modifying their approaches to make their expectations and explanations more clear. If a student does not grasp the concept with a verbal explanation, I try other things like a demonstration before letting him try it on his own. Sometimes I will just ask him what his preference is: "Would you like to try it or see me do it first?" Some are okay with trying it after I describe it and others feel better when they see me do it first.

Men learn in a linear and logical fashion. This is not to say that women are not logical; but rather that men use logic to decipher new information. They learn things in a step-by-step process, with a logical beginning, middle and end. They are willing to go out and learn using a trial-and-error method.

I heard about two sailing classes going on at the same time. One was a group of women and the other a group of men. The women started out on the dock talking and the guys just jumped into the boat and took off. They did their class out on the water and when they came back the women were still on the dock talking. The guys thought, "those women are just gossiping and cackling and it doesn't look like they are doing a sailing lesson at all!" What they didn't understand was that this was the most important part of the women's class because they needed to have all the components laid out for them: boat parts, how the boat works, reassurance that it won't capsize when it heels and so on. They needed to see the whole process and what they could expect to happen before they went out sailing.

4. SHE COMMUNICATES VERBALLY, HE IS NON-VERBAL.

This is where the fingernails-on-the-chalkboard-syndrome starts. She needs to talk out loud and sometimes repetitively about something in order to learn it and comprehend it. This is the exact opposite of men, who are, in the words of John Gray (author of *Men are From Mars and Women are From Venus*), cave dwellers. All of the male processing is done internally. Typically, they don't talk if they don't have to, and they don't talk until they are done processing. This can drive a woman absolutely crazy too, because she is looking for feedback and not getting any. This has to be one of the biggest struggles between men and women and that is why I have devoted an entire chapter to communication.

She verbalizes her feelings and her understanding or evaluation of things out loud. This is why women need to get together and talk. It's not just about gossiping; it is how they evaluate a problem and decide how to respond. It is not a quiet process. Guys, you really need to get this: women cannot learn without speaking through the process. The more she is able to speak about it, the better she understands. Some women need more talk time than others. So take it with a grain of salt.

And Ladies, believe it or not, men can go into their minds, think through all the scenarios and possibilities and then produce the output. Once they have processed a problem in their minds, they have the solution and they implement it. It's done .

The fire drill crisis happens when he suddenly announces (to her it is sudden), "Prepare to Tack!" If she is new to sailing and unaware of these terms, this announcement is taking her completely by surprise. It puts her in a panic because she isn't ready. The command comes across to her as being urgent, and if she doesn't act immediately something bad will happen. The feeling of panic causes her brain to shut down and now she has forgotten what she is supposed to do. And what is worse, she now fears that she is going to be yelled at for not doing things in a hurry. She is now sure she will probably do the wrong thing or grab the wrong line and make things worse. And sometimes she does get yelled at, which doesn't help the situation any.

This is close to home for me. These were my feelings and thoughts when I first started sailing. I was overwhelmed and unsure of myself. I couldn't think fast enough because I hadn't been given enough information in the first place. I was going through the motions without any real understanding. And it always felt like everything was life or death.

May I offer a suggestion to the non-communicative sailor? What is wrong with giving a little heads-up warning? How about saying, "Hey honey, we are going to need to Tack here soon, can you break away from what you are doing and start getting ready?" If she is still learning that will give her a few minutes to process and she will probably say out loud, "I think I need to get this line first and then do that." If she isn't sure, it will come across as a question rather than a statement. She is looking for a little confirmation and reassurance from you before she does it. All you need to do is agree. One word, "Yep" And now she is good to go!

Because she was given the time she needed to process and prepare, and that one word of reassurance that she is doing things correctly, tacking is not a frightening experience. It only takes a brief moment for her to be ready and she is happy, because now she is confident she is doing the right thing. Her need was met and she received that confirmation that she's got it.

I know some guys are grunting and groaning and going "Oh no, I'll go crazy with all that yakking." Here is the good news: just because this is how she learns does not mean that this will go on forever. Once she is confident in her skills and abilities, guess what? She doesn't need to do all that talking any more. Really, I promise. She just needs that positive verbal reinforcement as she is learning. If you just give her a bit of verbal confirmation as she talks, out loud, through the process, you will make her very happy and now she can have fun, too.

Women so often feel behind the gun because they are not given the opportunity in a boat full of cave-dwelling men to do their verbal processing. Too often they are either treated like they are stupid or are holding the class back. Or worse, the men just keep going and forget about her. They may then feel unable to do it because of the pressure to perform, or because she isn't getting it as quickly as the rest of the people on the boat. If anyone gets irritated with her she will either just shut down and quit or let the tears start to flow.

This scenario happens unnecessarily. It illustrates why private classes for couples are becoming more and more popular. When I teach one couple at a time, both the husband and I are rooting for the wife to succeed. She is allowed to talk all she wants, and she is allowed to practice all she needs to. Because we are here for her, we don't care how long it takes or how much we talk about it. With only two people on board, rather than a group setting, they both get more helm time, too. They are learning how to sail short-handed, which is a benefit since it will only be the two of them in the real world. It's a win-win situation.

If a husband is unwilling to take a couple's class, at the very least, the wife should get into a good women's program. Even guys often say they feel more comfortable with a female instructor, because now he can ask questions without the fear of someone thinking he is stupid. Ask away, I say. And I personally love "why" questions. If an instructor cannot tell you why, then they either don't know what they are doing or shouldn't be teaching.

5. SHE IS TEAM-ORIENTED, HE WANTS A CHAIN OF COMMAND.

Women are wired to seek fairness and equality. Men are wired to challenge and like to be challenged. Their approach to life is like playing King of the Hill. If there is a struggle for top position, he is more than willing to fight to prove he is King. It's about his virility! The alternative is unthinkable to him and affects his ego. He will fight until he wins the battle. A lot of men are not willing to take the back seat, particularly when it comes to sailing.

That is why you always see two male animals fighting it out to be head of the pack. The lions, the wolves, whatever; it's always about who is stronger to win and lead the females. Human males see themselves as the Knights in shining armor, fighting for the fair maiden. I know this is basic cave-man stuff. While we handle things in a more civilized manner today and in our culture, the underlying natural instincts remain.

In contrast, women are raised in an atmosphere where teamwork is emphasized. They want to help, nurture, work and play cooperatively. They are interested in being helpful, supportive and accommodating. She views a relationship as a partnership, where everyone is on equal footing.

When they go sailing, she views it as an opportunity for them to bond and work as a team. Men are raised to be more competitive, so there must be a pecking order on the boat. Only one person is in charge, giving orders, which means that there must be someone to obey the orders. There must be that Horatio Hornblower fantasy where he is the admiral of the ship.

It goes something like this: he's taking my sailing class to fulfill a fantasy he has had from childhood. He is standing straight and tall near the helm with his hands held behind his back, looking around and making his orders known, while he expects the crew (his wife) to carry them out. He imagines her saluting and everyone aboard running quickly at the captain's beck and call. Earth to Admiral Hornblower—it's time to snap out of it! You know it's never going to happen, not in this lifetime or on this boat, if you want her to keep sailing with you, that is. So get over it. You can be the captain and still try the team approach.

That whole fantasy requires crew to do the work from a submissive position. Men who are insecure in their masculinity will feel threatened by a woman who is competent at the helm and confident taking on "blue" jobs. They fear sharing, or worse, losing their position as captain.

This was really the reason Didier and I parted company. While I was striving for team-work, he thought I was relegating him to a submissive role. I made it clear to him from the day we met that I was captain. However, in my mind, this was to be a team effort. I knew I didn't know it all and could not do it all. I thought we had a good balance of responsibilities.

When there was a decision to make, I would ask his opinion. I valued his input. But in his mind, asking his advice meant that I was weak and incapable of making a decision. So I would sometimes have to just make the decision. That would make him feel devalued and he didn't like it. I felt like I couldn't win, but neither of us could clarify why we were struggling with making the decisions together. We did not have a solid foundation in our relationship in terms of communication, primarily because French was his dominant language.

This feeling that men have to compete for the top position makes working together on a boat a battle rather than a companionable sharing of tasks, skills, and responsibilities. The truth is that having a woman aboard who is as competent and capable as her partner means he does not have to do all the work. It means that they share the burdens and decisions, rather than him shouldering all the responsibility. Hey, that might even mean that he can relax a little and have fun with it (what a concept).

I have had some men on board who have had a very difficult time taking direction from me as a female captain, and even try to initiate a battle with me. This doesn't happen very often, but each time it does, I am still taken aback because I handle things with a feminine manner, a "let's work together" approach, rather than the masculine, "let's fight for top dog position."

On my boat, as with most boat owners, there is only one captain. Since I own the boat, I win! I find it disconcerting when an argument happens, as I do tend to fall into a passive roll when I feel threatened. This is more the feminine side of me. I will always do what ever it takes to feel safe when out on the water. Once at the dock, I am in a stronger position to hold my ground, but that is just the way I handle conflict. Men tend to be more aggressive (that testosterone thing), while women tend to be more passive, particularly when they feel physically threatened. I might add that I know other women who handle these problems completely differently.

Women are looking at creating a spirit of cooperation. They are willing to share the load. They are looking for a compromise rather than a battle. She thinks, "If you do this, and I do that, we will have it all covered." She doesn't want to be put down or treated as if she is incapable. She doesn't want to feel helpless or powerless. I'm sure she will tell you what things she is comfortable doing and what she is happy to relinquish to you.

There are many women who would happily assume a traditional role and have the guy go ahead and do all that manly stuff. She has no interest in learning mechanical or electrical engineering, and that is okay. If you are a woman like me, who likes a challenge, then the more you learn, the more confident you are, and that is okay, too. Give her the opportunity to decide how much wants to participate in handling and maintaining the boat. You will find a good division of labor if you talk it through, though there will still be many shared responsibilities.

Ladies, do you have enough knowledge to navigate home? To do rescue and M.O.B. procedures under both power and sail? Do you know how to tack, jibe and trim the sail properly? Can you hold a course? Anchor, dock or pick up a mooring if necessary? Can you do these things as either crew or helmsman? Can you call on the VHF for help and give a position of Longitude and Latitude from the GPS? If not, it is no wonder you are worried and concerned. You should be. Lack of knowledge and preparedness can cause the loss of lives.

Women cannot simply accept the role of galley wench, and men must allow their mates the opportunities to become confident sailors. It has nothing to do with being replaced as captain. Hey guys, remember that M.O.B. statistic? You want her to know what she is doing. It is for your own good. You can keep her in the dark, but when it's all over with, she gets the boat and the insurance money.

6. SHE NEEDS THE GAME PLAN, HE WILL PLAY AS IT COMES.

It is easier for a woman to understand what you are showing her on the chart, if you show the entire region first. In sailing classes, I show the chart with the whole State of Florida first, and then point out our region in relation to the whole state, then after that I turn to the chart that shows the Tampa Bay area, and finally, I will show the details of Boca Ciega Bay. Now it makes sense, because the ladies saw the big picture first.

As I have mentioned previously, if you only give a portion of the picture, a woman may be able to carry out a task, but she may not completely understand it or be able to duplicate it. She has to be given the overall picture or process first. When getting on a boat for the first time, she needs to know what it will look and feel like before she tries it, whereas a man is willing to gain his experience as he goes. He can learn it piecemeal and put it all together later.

When thinking about going cruising, she wants to know, "Where are we going? Are we going to the Bahamas or around the world?" Or, "To the San Juan Islands or Tahiti?" She may be willing to go on the shorter trip, but not so willing to make that ocean passage. He would rather say, "Let's just see how far we get." or "We will decide on the next destination later, we don't need to decide now." This will be unsettling to her.

I remember reading the book, *Gentlemen Never Sail to Weather, An Accidental Odyssey*, by Denton Moore. It's an entertaining story, about a couple that set out to sail to the Caribbean and four years later they had made a circumnavigation of the world. It had never been their plan to do so, and consequently there were quite a few adventures and misadventures along the way, because they weren't quite prepared to go the distance.

They did live through the ordeal, but not without a lot of mishaps. The story is told from his perspective, and he figured it out as they went, as most guys do. I would love to hear her side of the story. If you want a good laugh, read the book. You can learn a lot from the mistakes they could have avoided had they planned and been a little better prepared. It often takes both the female and male perspective—planning plus spontaneity—to make cruising work.

7. SHE WANTS TO KNOW WHY, HE WANTS TO KNOW HOW.

Now guys, you are going to have to help us out on this one because women really need to know *why* they are doing something so that they won't have to worry about the possibility of something bad happening. Women are always on a mission to feel safe. Being in control of our environment can give us a sense of security, but controlling others or taking charge is not usually the motive for our asking *why?*

I had a friend who told me that it annoys him when his wife asks him the question, *why?* because he felt that if she learned the answer to *why?*, she would want to try and take control. He took it as a challenge to his authority. I guess some women might do that, but I really don't think that is usually the motivation behind the question. Rather, she is more concerned that if something happens to him she wants to be able to get them both back to land safely. For most women, the attempt to take control is the farthest thing from her mind.

We want to know *why?* so that we can feel like we understand what is going on. I don't like being in the dark about things. I want to be able to know how to do something if necessary. I am certainly not plotting in the back of my mind, "once I know this I can take control of the vessel and rule the seven seas!" I just don't see this as being valid.

Sometimes, when things just don't make sense, the *why?* questions are for clarification. Answering the *why?* question for women can generate reassurance. Women are going to be comforted by understanding. It's a confirmation that things are still safe. For me, anything to do with the electrical system is a mystery and thus intimidating. There is the fear of danger and the worry of a costly mistake. So I will question "why do this instead of that?" I won't just go messing with something electrical. A man, on the contrary, will ask "how does this work?" and then try to figure it out.

Everything I have learned about diesel engines came as a result of problems that happened. Most of the women's sailing seminars and conferences offer diesel and/or out board engine classes. Women don't want to wait for the crisis to learn. I don't blame them. That is when the panic and freaking out set in.

Now, in contrast, when the guy seeks to understand something, it is to achieve an end result, not merely alleviate anxiety. He wants to know *how* the diesel engine works so he can figure out what is wrong with it. The end result is that now he can fix it and keep the engine running smoothly.

Please, ladies, don't ask *why?* when you are in the middle of a problem or a crisis. If someone is telling you to do something unusual in an urgent voice, do it and don't ask questions. They wouldn't be telling you if there wasn't an important reason for doing it. There isn't time for an explanation in the middle of a crisis. Wait until after the crisis is over, and then ask. There should be an explanation as to what happened and you should be able to feel free to ask questions after things are back under control.

8. SHE WILL BE NON-RESPONSIVE IN A CRISIS, HE WILL TRY ANYTHING.

In times of crisis or unknown situations, women will tend to do nothing; you might call it the "deer-in-the-headlights syndrome." She will probably hand off the situation or relinquish her role if she isn't sure what to do, or if things seem too overwhelming. She worries she may cause further problems or damage by doing the wrong thing.

Guys are just the opposite. In times of crisis, he will tend to try anything rather than nothing to respond to the situation, even if he isn't sure of the outcome. He figures doing something is better than doing nothing. This is an extreme difference of gender responses.

A crisis creates a situation in which the woman may feel that she is being yelled at. This is because a man will see a problem and then start troubleshooting. Since she doesn't understand what is being asked of her, she feels that he is yelling at her, while in reality he doesn't know what to do either. He is just willing to keep trying different things until he gets things back under control. This conflict intensifies if he keeps changing his mind when things aren't working for him. He doesn't have time to explain himself.

I remember my response to helping dock the boat when I sailed on the forty foot IOR race boat with my boyfriend, Jack. I would wait for him to tell me to jump off the boat to the dock, even though I knew when to go. I had done it enough times, but I would still wait to be told where to tie the line, because I wasn't confident enough at the time to trust myself. I also worried that I would do something wrong and then get yelled at.

I had been teaching a couple how to reef the sails on their own boat a couple of years ago. As we were heading home, suddenly we heard the worst noise coming from the engine. The wife immediately handed the helm over to her husband, who tried to throttle up more, thinking he could hurry and get us back to the dock. Of course, he quickly realized that was a bad idea and shut the engine down. He stayed at the helm because she was completely unwilling to take it back now that there was a problem. So he got a chance to learn how to sail the boat back to the dock, not that he had many other options. She and I got the sails back up in a hurry (a good reminder why you shouldn't clean the lines up and put the sails away until you are back at the dock).

Neither one of them had ever sailed to the dock before. But they had polar opposite responses to the prospect of doing something new. The husband and I were excited about the prospect of taking on this challenge, but the wife was almost holding her breath in panic. Everything worked out well and we looked really cool sailing into the slip. Now they both feel more confident from this experience, and know that even if they lose their engine, they can still get back to safety. Learning the hard way is often a confidence builder, but their handling of the situation perfectly illustrates how men and women react differently to stress.

9. SHE TENDS TO OVERREACT, HE TENDS TO UNDER-REACT.

I will admit that my fears contributed to some of the petty arguments between Didier and myself. I recall writing in my journal that Didier was agitated with me for freaking out over what he thought was nothing. I saw a couple of different ships on the horizon while we were making one of our trips to the Bahamas. I couldn't tell what I was looking at and I got worried that we might be in danger of a collision. If I had known what I was looking at, I wouldn't have needed his help. He had been below sleeping, but rather than taking a moment to reassure me, he got annoyed instead.

Had he taken just a few minutes to explain to me why he wasn't worried about a collision, it would have completely diminished my fears (however silly they seemed) and permitted me to continue my night watch without the unnecessary hours of worry. Now I understand that I overreacted because I lacked understanding, which created fear. The more I have learned, the less I tend to overreact to situations.

I see this on the boat a lot with female students. The first day we go out, she is worried about colliding with every single boat she sees. Once she understands how to evaluate the situation and determine which ones are potential problems and which ones aren't, she relaxes. This applies to most sailing skills.

I will never forget one of my confidence-building experiences. I had invited a group of friends out sailing for the 4th of July during the time I was working toward getting my captain's license and certifications to teach. I warned everyone to bring rain jackets because you can count on a daily afternoon rain in Florida. I saw the dark clouds rolling in and told everyone we needed to head back. Even though everyone was disappointed, I got the sails down and the anchor ready to go and was heading back to the harbor. The storm was not one of our typical afternoon storms. It was packed with severe winds, lighting and hail. Suddenly we were in five-foot seas and the rain was coming down so hard it was as though we were in fog. We had minimal visibility for a while.

It was chaos. There was one girl throwing up over the side. Three people went below with my dog who was barking frantically. One guy standing in the companionway wouldn't shut up and a woman got on the VHF radio and yelled May-Day. I had the guy with the most experience next to me on the helm. I kept him there, figuring he was stronger at holding the boat into the wind than I would be. I immediately started putting people in life jackets and reassuring everyone that we would be okay.

It seemed like this storm lasted forever, and it certainly was longer than the typical summer storm. Later, after we returned to the dock, everyone told me that they knew we would be okay, because they watched me respond calmly. The next day, I found out that we were in thirty-five mph sustained winds, with gusts to sixty. I have to confess that while everyone saw me as calm and confident, on the inside I was just as concerned and worried as everyone else. I just didn't let anyone see it. Their confidence in me was as a result of how I projected myself to them. I had stayed calm and didn't overreact to the situation.

I use this story to illustrate a point. Guys may appear as if they are under-reacting, but often it is a façade of tranquility that they project as captain or helmsman to keep everyone else calm. Next time, instead of accusing your mate of being unconcerned, thank him for keeping calm.

One obstacle to a man's ability to listen to his mate is that she has the propensity to overreact. She may say "I have a bad feeling about this" but because he doesn't have the same gut instincts, or because she has "bad feelings" about a lot of things that turn out to be nothing he ignores it. Remember, just because she overreacts doesn't mean disaster isn't imminent!

There are countless stories I could tell you about trusting my instincts, but I will summarize them in this way: every single time I went against my intuitions about a situation, I regretted it. Every time I got talked into sailing when I looked at the weather and felt it was risky, every time I had a bad feeling and ignored it, and every time people would push and beg for me to do something that I felt would be a mistake but did it anyway, I regretted it. Even though they said they were willing to accept the consequences, they were not. Either the weather would beat us up or they would beat me up because they were unhappy. So heed my advice: better to regret a missed trip or a rendezvous with others at a particular place or time, than to be frightened half to death and then, on top of it, have to hear the dreaded words, "I told you so."

I have been asked by men, "How do I know the difference between her legitimate fears and her overreacting or freaking out? How do I know when to listen to her gut instinct?" I think the answer is to ask, what is her experience and knowledge in that situation? Often what would be considered an irrational fear is linked to lack of understanding. Sit down together and look at all the facts. How much fear of the unknown is mixed into her decision? Is this a time when she has a lot of experience but feels uncertain anyway? Come to an agreement; make the decision together. Lastly, determine whether it is worth suffering the consequences if the risk-taker overrules the more conservative partner.

One last consideration if you're still wondering why she's freaking out: could it be that she didn't get the whole picture? Like when my boyfriend called me to come up on deck, in the middle of the night, to take the helm because he needed to take a reef. He waited until the storm had already hit us. I was still groggy. All of a sudden I was thrown into a crisis, in the middle of a dark and stormy night. Hey, who wouldn't get a little freaked out? I needed a little more warning, or at least some information so I didn't think we were sinking.

Telling a woman to just "stop freaking out" or that you have it under control without telling her why she doesn't need to worry, doesn't usually help. But, ladies, sometimes you will just have to trust him and take him at his word when he tells you that he has it under control. Guys, if you promise to explain later, and keep that promise when things are back under control, she will overreact in a stressful situation less and less.

10. SHE IS THE CARETAKER AND SUPPORTER, HE IS THE PROTECTOR AND PROVIDER.

As the caretaker, she needs to make even confined quarters comfortable and pleasant. She takes pleasure in providing creature comforts. Adding things that are pleasing to the senses is her contribution to making a place a home. Having a cockpit table or throw pillows in the salon may not be important to him, but they are to her. Women don't want to feel like they are camping.

A man, as you recall, is the Knight in shining armor; he has an innate need to work to support and protect his loved ones. He always has protection in the back of his mind, even if it comes out differently than she expects. To her, he is always tinkering around with something on the boat. To him, he is making sure that the boat will get them back to the harbor safely.

Traditionally, men have always been the protectors and providers of the home, village, or tribe. It doesn't matter if a man is on a boat or on a farm or in a cave. He is always thinking in the back of his mind about all the possible things that could go wrong, and how he will respond. A woman may be thinking about safety issues, but she's doing it out loud. Remember that verbal/non-verbal thing? She can't hear him solving problems—she has no idea what is happening in that cave! She comes up with all sorts of reasons why he isn't talking to her. "Is he mad at me? What did I do wrong? Did I say something to upset him?" All her questions are relational, and have nothing to do with what is really important to him. She would feel so much safer if she knew that he was working quietly behind the scenes on things ultimately result in her safety and comfort at sea.

To a woman, it seems that all her man does is tinker on the boat. Actually, all that annoying tinkering he is doing is really fine-tuning the boat to assure that things will go smoothly. So ladies, applaud him for going down into the bilges, and sitting at the anchorage an extra day so he can fix that 'thingamajig' or 'whatchamacallit'. You would rather put up with that than the alternative: having the engine shut down just as you are coming in through a breakwater, where the water churns like a washing machine and the current is starting to push you backwards toward the rocks!

11. SHE MAKES DECISIONS EMOTIONALLY, HE MAKES DECISIONS LOGICALLY.

She will decide if it is okay to do something if she feels safe, if she feels good about it, or if she feels like it will be fun. If she has a bad feeling, chances are she is either not going to do it or put up a fight. Women are more apt to listen to their gut instincts than men are. Men, however, operate from the logical side of the brain, and they can get themselves into trouble because they don't listen to the gut.

Earlier, I gave the example of coming into an anchorage at night, and said it was something I would not have chosen to do. The important thing to me, is to have an escape route if I am going to attempt to do something that I think is daring or dangerous. If I know I have an alternate plan, I am more open to attempting something that seems risky. That's because my emotions play into my decision-making.

Don't be too quick to dismiss a woman's instincts and write them off as an overreaction. Very often that little knot in her stomach can help you avoid some terrible experiences. Not to mention that dreaded experience at the end of it all, when you hear those four words that make a guy's heart sink, "I told you so." It's called women's intuition, and it's not imaginary.

In the man's case, he is willing to forge ahead even if he isn't sure. Not one of the guys on *Maya*, for example, was saying, "I don't think this is a good idea." It was only me saying that. The guys kept working, looking with the night scope, and checking the charts. They were going back and forth, reading the computer chart to see where we were. They were examining evidence and following a logical sequence. I was doing the same things, but I think for different reasons. I needed to be reassured that they were doing the right thing. Hearing those waves crashing on the shore and not seeing them caused no small amount of distress for me.

Again, who is to say which method is better? A woman changes her mind like she changes her shoes, sometimes making decisions based on a whim. But in a crisis, she might be able to "feel" the correct course of action. A man will continue on a steady course, based on hard evidence, despite fear or uncertainty and get his vessel to safety, but he also might ignore a nagging uncertainty that results in disaster. So many of these issues are resolved when each partner appreciates the other's approach and the two reach equilibrium.

12. SHE BLAMES HERSELF, HE BLAMES EVERYONE AND EVERYTHING ELSE.

Not all docking classes go as planned. The following story illustrates what happens when someone freezes up. If a woman doesn't know what to do, she may become paralyzed with the fear of something worse happening, and then actually cause this thing to happen. And someone has to take the blame.

There was an older couple onboard who had had no experience on boats prior to their class with me. I had an engine hoist on the stern of my boat for my outboard motor , which stuck out a little bit, but it had never been a problem in docking classes in the past. The wind was blowing us onto the dock, so when we were trying to leave, the woman, who was at the helm, started having problems. I kept telling her to stop the boat, but she was not responding by throttling down. Even though everything had been explained to her, more than once, her brain shut down when the situation became problematic. She did not understand that "stop" meant that she needed to throttle down and put the engine in neutral. In an attempt to help, the husband started pushing the bow away from the pilings, which was actually making matters worse, because it was forcing the stern, and thus the engine hoist, against the pilings even more. The hoist bent against a piling before we could break free.

The whole time she just stood at the helm frozen. The minute we were free and I was able to take control of the helm, the husband came running back to the cockpit and blamed me for the mishap. He yelled at me, "It wasn't her fault!" She looked at him and yelled, "Yes it was!" Knowing what I know about gender traits, all I could do was chuckle. A man will blame anyone standing nearby, and a woman will blame herself.

We were able to regroup and eventually go out for more docking practice. She was shocked when I asked her to take the helm. She could not believe that I would even let her get back on the boat after what happened, let alone the helm, but I told her it's like falling off a horse; you need to get back on and try again right away and keep going until you're successful. If you don't, you will never do it again. In the end, she did an excellent job and the damage was minimal—both to the boat and to their relationship!

13. SHE NEEDS TIME TO PROCESS INFORMATION, HE MAKES DECISIONS QUICKLY.

A woman needs to make sure that she is making the right decision. Stepping out into the unknown can be unsafe. Here is the lengthy process: first she will need to discuss all the possibilities. She is slow and careful, especially if there is any hint of danger. Remember, she doesn't like to push the limits. Next, she will list all the pros and cons. Finally, she will narrow down the best options until she can make a choice. Then she will second-guess herself, and maybe even change her mind, but eventually, with a little prodding she will arrive at a conclusion or decision.

Sometimes a person's hesitation comes from worrying about making the wrong decision. Indecision can be a big hindrance to both men and women. Women typically gain their confidence by achieving small successes. With each new accomplishment, she becomes willing to go on to the next step. Don't forget, she needs verbal reassurance and gentle coaching through any learning or decision-making process.

Here are the contrasting responses in a classroom setting: some women will approach learning to sail with the attitude that they probably cannot do this, while the guy will believe he can from the start. She is terrified of docking the boat the first time, while he will just jump right in there and try it, whether he knows what to do or not. She seems slower because she needs the big picture up front, but he can learn one step at a time.

She needs to be coached into doing something new, even more so if it looks dangerous. It is sometimes the very same danger she fears that enticed him in the first place! In a dangerous situation, he is quicker to make a decision and will deal with the consequences, even if it he later finds out he was wrong. I don't think men will take unnecessary or uncalculated risks—they don't want to die either—but they are quicker to say, "Let's just try it. We can always turn back."

While getting ready for a passage, she will look at the weather and feel that it might not be a good idea to leave today, while he says "let's just go and get there. So what if there is a little wind?" But we must remember that this is a team effort. When a man is taking a woman beyond her comfort zone, he is asking for trouble. By agreeing that there must be a consensus before leaving the anchorage or marina, both people are leaning on the others' decision-making process. You will have less conflict by finding the compromise.

14. SHE MULTI-TASKS, HE DOES TASKS SEQUENTIALLY.

If you looked into the brain of a woman versus that of a man, it would look like a computer screen with many windows open and all running at the same time. She can have a spreadsheet open with lists of all the items in every locker, how many of each kind of canned good they have, how much toilet paper is left and it's location on the boat, etc. She will also have a document open to show her when she will run out of those items, and in what city she thinks they may be when it is time to restock. She might also be writing a letter, using the calculator and looking at a calendar. All these windows and programs would be running at the same time and she would be moving back and forth between them, without missing a beat.

I know this about her because I am doing the exact same thing right now. I'm online checking email, I've got my program open for this book, the power point for changing and editing my seminar notes and I'm online balancing my check book and uploading forms from the U.S. copyright web site so that I can make sure my book is protected before sending it out to be edited. I've also got the copy machine running to print up some things for an upcoming seminar and I'm ready to start another load of laundry.

Most guys will think they are doing well if they get one thing done at

a time and it gets done well. Who is to say which is the right or wrong approach? It is what it is, a part of our genetic makeup. Sometimes neither of us can understand how the other ever gets anything done! I don't think I would ever get everything accomplished in the time that I have, if I only did one thing at a time. And most guys would be pulling their hair out if they had five or six things going at once, as women often do.

Ladies, because a guy gets focused on only one thing at a time it is easy for him to forget what it is that you asked of him. If he gets nagged, belittled, or fussed-at when he forgets your request, he is less likely to be responsive in the way that you want him to be. Just like you are asking him to be patient with you while you are learning new information, you need to give him a break on those little things that he forgets. Ask him again, and know that you may have to ask three times before you get what you need. The magic trick is to ask, even if you have already asked him repeatedly, as if you are asking him the first time.

The real key to success when dealing with each other's gender differences can be summed up using the golden rule: Treat each other the way you want to be treated. These descriptions may not match up with you or your mate perfectly, but they are true often enough to be instructive. Instead of looking at the exceptions, try finding the things that do fit you and your partner. Use the list as an opening for dialog and an opportunity to communicate about your relationship and reconfirm your love for each other.

TWO ON A BOAT HOW TO KEEP IT AFLOAT

SEVEN

COMMUNICATION - COMMUNICATION - COMMUNICATION

Because women are verbal beings they usually don't have a problem talking about it. When the guy who is the cave dweller doesn't give a verbal response, one of two things will happen.

VERBAL & NON-VERBAL METHODS THAT WORK FOR BOTH

The word assume, can be broken down into three little words. Do I need to spell it out? When it comes to communication there is no room on a boat to assume anything. This is the major cause of conflict between couples, but can also be a problem between any two people. Without concise, two-way communication, there is no meeting of minds and we call it a breakdown in communication.

The conversation might go something like this: she yells back to him from the bow, but, unfortunately, she has her back to him, so he doesn't hear a word she says. Meanwhile, he has the engine roaring in his ears and can't hear her say, "Look, there is a rock ahead over there." He just sees her pointing and because they have not distinguished hand signals for "look over there" versus "go over there," he heads right to the rock and hits it.

He starts yelling, "Why didn't you tell me there was a rock over there?"

She angrily retorts, "I did tell you there was a rock over there!"

"I didn't hear you!" He shouts.
She comes back with, "Didn't you see me pointing at it?"
He responds, "I thought you wanted me to go over there!"

In the example above, can you see the assumptions each person made? This is the kind of communication, or should I say lack thereof, that first gets us into big trouble and next causes relationships to fall apart. Never, ever, make any assumptions! Poor communication can happen between men and women, two men, or two women, so this isn't just a gender issue. It's not a "he said, she said" thing. It's a failure of two people to meet in the middle.

There is only one assumption you can ever make on a boat. I know I just said "never," but there are always exceptions to rule. So here it is, the one assumption you may make: If someone didn't answer or acknowledge you, then you can assume he did not hear you! If you literally don't see eye-to-eye—meaning if you can't make eye contact—chances are that there will a breakdown in communication.

Because women are verbal beings they usually don't have a problem talking about it. When the guy who is the cave dweller doesn't give a verbal response, one of two things will happen. She will either keep repeating herself, which drives him crazy, or she will just give up and get annoyed or angry that he is not talking to her. The guys in my classes always tell me, "I got it, so why do I have to say it out loud?" The answer is: you have to say it so that she can hear it! She needs to know that what you heard is what she meant. I truly believe that this contributes in a big way to the anxiety that women experience on boats.

Because the guy is not communicating and she doesn't really understand the situation, she is unsure of what the outcome will be. Then the *what if's* start rolling through her mind and the worst-case scenarios consume her. He may have things completely under control but she doesn't know it unless he verbally conveys it to her. And she doesn't need to hear a condescending comment like, "I've got it under control." She needs to understand why he feels that it is under control.

This is where he can help her by giving her some information. Withholding information causes her stress. Of course, she also needs

to understand that in a critical situation his comment, "I've got it under control," will have to suffice until later, when they've gotten through the situation. The important thing is to discuss it; beforehand is better, but at least go over things after the fact so that you can both grow from the experience rather than leaving it as a source of contention or fodder for a future argument.

SPEAK THE SAME LANGUAGE

First, have everyone on the boat speak the same language when talking to each other. Second, don't use layman's terms with new people, and then be surprised when they don't understand proper nautical terminology.

This was one of the biggest hurdles for me when I started sailing. At first, Jack didn't ask me to do anything. I was just along for the ride. If he did want me to do something, he would only give a brief explanation, something like, "Pull on this line when I tell you." I would try to do what I was told, but never understood the whole process. Then when things got crazy and he would yell, "Sheet in!" I had no clue what a sheet was or where he was telling me to put it.

When he finally did start using the right terminology with me, I felt like he was talking a foreign language. Remember my example? "Head up!" he would shout. I would respond with, "My head is up, but which way do you want me to turn?" If he said, "Turn to Port," I would ask, "Is that left or right?" How simple it would have been to resolve some of the communication problems; all I needed was the opportunity to learn the new language beforehand.

The jargon of sailing is like that of any new language, sport, or profession. You must first learn the vocabulary before you can even attempt to put a sentence together. We get onto a boat and then we suddenly can't understand each other. When was that foundation laid? Oh, that's the problem; there never was a foundation, so no wonder you can't communicate. Hmmm…maybe you should get the basics down first. (See the chapter on the Foundation of Sailing.) Beginners, read a book, take an online class, and work on this before you get your boat or take the on-the-water sailing class. Won't your partner be surprised when you show up talking like a pro?

There are several reasons you hear couples yelling on the boat. One is that the helmsman really doesn't know what he is asking the crew to do, because he doesn't fully know himself. I have found some of the guys who were guilty of yelling from the helm, when put in a crew position, didn't know what to do when it came to things like docking. If they couldn't do it in the first place, how could they ask others to do it?

I have to chuckle when I hear them try to blame me, because although they told me that they understood when I reviewed procedures, they either didn't understand and wouldn't admit it, or they didn't think through the process and go to plan 'B' when plan 'A' didn't work. This is why we always need to do a follow-up session at the end of practicing a new skill. It helps to remind everyone of things they forgot and clarify anything that was misunderstood. Then just move on; don't dwell on old stuff and place blame. Just learn the lesson and get over it.

I promise that if you learn a lesson from every situation that doesn't work out the way that you expected, you will quickly become more competent and confident in your abilities. Rather than being left feeling upset with each other, you will have worked together to find solutions, and together you will be better equipped should that situation ever arise again.

When we get into the docking and anchoring section, I will talk more about what works and what doesn't. These are the two areas, which cause the most conflict on the boat. Again, because there are more problems when it comes to docking and anchoring than anything else, I have devoted a whole chapter to them.

Another reason why there may be confusion and yelling is that the person giving a command didn't get a verbal acknowledgement from the crew. If you've sailed at all, you know that if you are standing at the helm with your crew on the bow, you cannot hear what he says to you, especially if his back is to you! Even on a twenty- eight-foot boat, the helmsman cannot hear his crew's response. Eye contact and a verbal acknowledgement, or clear non-verbal signal, are crucial to eliminating the "I told you – No you didn't" argument. If there isn't a clear response from the other person, don't make the assumption that they heard you.

MASCULINE VS. FEMININE COMMUNICATION

She is saying it; he is analyzing it. That sums it up pretty well, but here is a short list of other differences in the way men and women communicate. It is easy to see how these two will get their wires crossed!

Her priorities are the relationships, not the mechanics. She communicates on matters of the heart; she talks through a situation without there having to be a final decision. Sometimes she will talk about a whole variety of things that have happened during the day in no particular order. He goes into his cave to analyze, evaluate, arrive at a conclusion, and make a decision. She needs to just vent, which can make him crazy because he is a logical thinker. To him there should be a beginning, middle, and end. Because her venting doesn't necessarily have these elements, it leaves him lost and confused. He doesn't feel that it is necessary to say something out loud because he is acting on it. She needs to hear it to have it confirmed. Because she is the verbal processor, she doesn't always recognize his efforts since he is not saying it.

This topic is so vast that John Grey has multiple books and tapes on it. I am only tapping into a fraction of the subject matter, but I hope that it will get everyone thinking about the many differences in communication styles.

Conflict happens when each partner is trying to influence the other and get the other to conform to his or her way of thinking and acting. It just isn't going to happen. Just as the leopard cannot change his spots and the zebra cannot change her stripes, men and women are of a different nature, so it is only with understanding and willingness that they can adapt and adjust their attitudes and behaviors to begin pursuing a common goal. Here's a good example of a win-win situation: when he puts forth a few words, she is reassured; once she is reassured and reaches understanding, she talks less. A small effort can reap big rewards.

TWO-WAY COMMUNICATION

Using this simple tool, responding consistently to each other, would cut down by ninety percent, and possibly eliminate, misunderstandings and arguments on a boat. Okay, maybe that is a bit optimistic, but I do believe that it will fix or diminish a majority of the problems.

I love having guys in my class with a military background because the get the concept of two-way communication. When the captain gives instructions, the crew responds with "Aye, aye." Meaning, I heard you (the first aye) and I understand (the second aye). There is always a response to the captain's orders. This should be mandatory on a boat—it can save your life!

Now you don't have to go around saying "Aye, aye" all the time. But by repeating back or parroting what you were told, you give the person who gave the command (or request, direction, instruction, etc.) the knowledge that you not only heard him, but that you are acting on it. There is also room for further clarification if necessary. It certainly saves a lot of time and heartache in the long run.

Keep in mind that it doesn't necessarily have to be long and drawn out. I remind women that the commands given by men are typical of a cave-dweller. His communication is short, sweet and to the point. He uses as few words as possible. He might even consider things like a grunt and nod of the head an acceptable verbalization. I know you guys hate to state the obvious, but it really helps to verbally reassure her with actual words that there is no misunderstanding and that everything is still okay. Now, I know I'm exaggerating, but I mean no offense. In fact, I actually agree with keeping the communication concise and to-the-point. Sometimes the captain doesn't have time for lengthy explanations, but needs to use terse requests to get the job done.

I may not have time to tell the helmsman that there is a crab pot that he is bearing down on and if he does not head up immediately he is going to run over it. So I might just quickly say, "Head up, now!" Three

words versus twenty-five words. By the time I have finished with that long, drawn-out explanation about the crab pot, the line would already be fouled and then we would have bigger problems. Do you see why one can't always get an explanation first?

So next time someone tells you to do something—and hurry—stop questioning him and just do it, with the understanding that there is a reason for the sudden change in instructions. Once you are out of the situation you can ask, "What just happened?" But don't start arguing and demanding the explanation right then and there. Sometimes you just need to trust that person, and the explanation will follow.

Sensible people don't usually make erratic demands unless they have a good reason for it. On my boat, I always tell people, "Just do what you are told and I promise I will explain it after we are clear of the problem." And I always keep that promise. A couple should make an agreement ahead of time about how to handle this. He needs her quick response, and she needs to know why. They must compromise. She needs to delay her *why?* questions and he has to be willing to explain later. If this has been established, there is no argument necessary.

The biggest trouble I have gotten myself into when teaching a class is accepting someone's word when they tell me they know how to sail. I then expect them know their points of sail, and know which way to turn the boat and know the right things to say. Next thing you know, we are having problems because there are some gaps in this person's knowledge or ability. The best policy is not to assume anything. It won't hurt someone to hear the material again. And if you are in a sailing class, put that ego away—there just isn't enough room on the boat for you and that big ego. Try not to get irritated when someone tells you something you already know. Just acknowledge the information and go on with your business.

NON-VERBAL COMMUNICATION

Human beings communicate using words, hand gestures, facial expressions and posture (body language). The non-verbal forms of communication are often just as effective at conveying a person's thoughts and feelings as verbal communication. The key is, it must still be a two-way communication. We discussed earlier the importance of speaking the same language when on a boat. Using correct words and commands makes a huge difference. With the "head up" example, it is important to know that we are talking about heading upwind as opposed to going up the mast. The same is true of non-verbal communication: we must agree on what signals or gestures mean so that we can be understood.

Hand signals can be very useful when docking and anchoring, a situation where the person on the bow may not be within earshot of the person at the helm. If I were to point with one-finger verses pointing with my whole hand, would you know what I was telling you? Would you be able to tell the difference between the two gestures? The meaning of the gestures must be agreed upon before they can be used. For instance, one finger pointing is universal for, "Look." Using your whole hand, with fingers pointing the same direction, means "Go there." There is a big difference between "look" and "go." It may mean the difference between avoiding the rocks or running aground.

When making a gesture, you must be sure that you have eye-contact, or the communication will not be two-way. If you are at the bow and your back is to the helmsman, you have no idea if he was looking at you when you pointed. You can't assume. By looking back at the helmsman and getting a nod or thumbs-up confirmation, there is no doubt that you were understood.

You should know by now that everyone on the dock or in the anchorage is listening to hear how the new arrivals speak to each other. When a couple uses hand signals that they have agreed upon ahead of time, they will look like they are experienced because it is a quiet and controlled operation. They will be the envy of the anchorage. People will think they've been sailing together forever and it could be the first time they've done it. I challenge you to try it and see what I mean!

NEGATIVE NON-VERBAL

Then there is that all-too-familiar look of disgust when you have made a mistake and the other person on the boat shows you his displeasure. When Jack would get aggravated with me for turning the wrong way (again), he knew better than to yell. Many people had told me how verbally abusive he was on race boats, but he kept his promise and never yelled at me—out loud, that is! Unfortunately, it didn't eliminate all of my tears, because I would get that look of disgust from him and feel worthless. Because I never really understood what I was doing, it was impossible for me to always get it right. I would revert to just doing what I was told, and avoid being at the helm.

That look of disappointment, irritation or displeasure can hold someone back from making progress just as much as hearing the words "you're stupid." I've had students come to me after taking their basic sailing class from someone like that. They were very nervous about getting out on the water, because they didn't want to get "that look" reminding them without words how badly they had messed up. Now ladies, in case you thought only guys are guilty of this, here is the contribution you make to kill his ego. Everyone knows that the worst thing you can say to a guy is, "I told you so." Well, that little look you do, with the eyebrows up and a little cock of the head, takes the wind from his sails, so to speak. If you don't like that non-verbal put-down, you cannot give it to him either.

To those who have gotten "the look:" sometimes even instructors will reveal with a facial expression (or worse) how displeased they are, which really isn't fair. I make a promise never to do so. People who take a class on a boat that has a tiller and then step onto a boat with a wheel will inevitably turn the wrong way. I call it *tiller mentality.* When I know people have learned on a tiller, they get even more TLC to help them remember the correct way to turn, not a glare when they make a mistake. My rule is that day one is the introduction to sailing and my students can do no wrong. Or rather, I make it an environment where it's safe to make mistakes. How can anyone be expected to do it right the first time? So we mess it up first and see that everything will be okay. I have no expectations on day one. Without the pressure to perform, they feel successful on their first day, and it's a blast instead of being scary.

When a student can see they can't break anything or do anything horribly wrong, they can relax and enjoy the learning process. I don't see how some instructors can get upset with students for doing something incorrectly when they haven't had the time to learn it first. It's like punishing a baby for not clapping his hands the first time you show him. It's ludicrous.

If you are in the beginning stages of learning to sail, don't beat yourself if you aren't doing it perfectly yet. Everyone needs time to figure it out, some more than others. Proficiency comes with repetition, and we learn the best lessons from our mistakes. We need to be able speak up and say, "I don't know," without being afraid of getting "the evil eye." When someone doesn't understand what is being asked of them, they need to feel comfortable to let someone know. It is the instructor's job to clarify and sometimes restate the information in a different way, not to belittle.

THE THOUGHT PROCESS

Learning the thought process while sailing is one of the biggest things that takes women from deck fluff to skipper material. It will most definitely give them a feeling of safety and understanding.

When I was sailing in Seattle, I had a good friend, Jack (not the same Jack), who had sold his boat to a guy who was interested in racing the boat. The new owner wanted my friend to teach him how to skipper the boat in a race. A group of us went to meet this guy, Al, on his boat in the San Juan Islands. My friend sat back near the helm with Al and started coaching him out loud. Throughout the race I eavesdropped and heard Jack tell Al things like, "Look over there, do you see the wind? We need to make our way over there where that puff is." He kept talking to him and gave him every strategy and thought that was going through his mind to help Al to be able to make good decisions.

Finally, I had discovered the guys' secrets to decision-making and I could see how they were figuring out what to do next. It was access into the secret cave! But when learning to sail, everyone should get this. Because men are doing all the processing internally, she never learns all the things that are going on in his mind before he makes a decision and blurts out a command.

A good friend of mine, in Maine, is a textbook case of the "man from Mars." This is not a bad thing, mind you; Frank is a great guy and I really like him. He has a beautiful forty-two-foot Vagabond, *Harvest Moon*, on which he does charters in the summer. Frank once told me, "I don't have time to tell her what is going on in my mind. I have so many little things that I am looking at, and considering, that I couldn't get the words out quick enough."

Aha! This is the part of the process that is causing women to feel fear and panic. She wonders, "Why is he doing that? What is going on? I don't understand!" It may be that her male sailing partner doesn't know how to explain what she should be looking for, and how to make those instant decisions.

What is the thought process? That running dialogue, moment-by-moment, play-by-play breakdown of what's going on with the wind and the boat, is worth the price of private lessons, if you can find a captain or instructor who can teach it to you. Once you understand the wind, and learn how to make good decisions based on its direction and speed, this is such an easy sport. I think sometimes people make it far more complicated than it needs to be.

I'm sure you are by now connecting the dots and can see how so much of what happens on a boat is about communicating clearly. It's about learning to work together as a team. In fact, it's such a good team-building exercise that corporations often send their workers on sailing expeditions to help them improve their cooperation and build on their strengths. Practice, good communication and a series of small successes will result in confidence. When we build each other up, then it's a win-win situation for everyone.

We are all more responsive and happy to try or do almost anything when we receive even a little positive reinforcement. Give what you would like to receive. If you want him to be patient with you, give him the same consideration. Guys, if you want her to sail to the ends of the earth with you, show her how much you care about her feelings and allow her to learn her way. And don't forget to speak up! Most commands and responses on boats require only speaking one or two words. It's not that difficult, but makes a world of difference for everyone on board.

EIGHT

THE YELLING FACTOR
TO YELL OR NOT TO YELL

There is a difference between yelling AT and yelling TO. In men's defense there are times when raising your voice is very important for safety and shouldn't be taken as if they are yelling AT.

INCLUDING SEVEN REASONS FOR RAISING YOUR VOICE

Should there ever be yelling on a boat? Sometimes? Is there really a time when yelling is acceptable? Are there times when yelling is necessary? When is it never right to yell? What is the right answer? When is it appropriate to yell and when is it not?

Eighty-four percent of the women polled said that yelling is their number one complaint about being on a boat. I think it is an important issue to address directly. Hang on guys—I'm coming to your defense on this in a few minutes. I say "guys" because it is often men doing the yelling, but I'm sure there are also female yellers out there to whom my words apply. There are many times when yelling is not only appropriate, but it may even be necessary to save lives. So let's look at when it's not okay to yell and when it is.

Feeling overwhelmed or unsure causes tears in women and yelling in men. I can't tell you how many times I have had men come up to me after my seminars and tell me, "Josie, I can tell you why men yell." I always say, "Please enlighten me, because I really don't know." The answer is the same every time. "It's because they don't know what they are doing." Of all people, it has been men who have informed me that when men yell it is because they don't know what to do. Straight from the horse's mouth!

The yeller thinks that by yelling he can give an appearance of knowledge, authority, or even superiority. Consider the tendency of people to raise their voices when speaking to those who don't understand their language. They yell thinking that speaking louder is somehow going to create understanding. The yeller thinks the miscommunication is the crew's fault, not their own. The truth is that the captain is ultimately responsible and cannot blame the crew.

Yelling usually does not make a person look smarter or more experienced. I have to tell you that most people think the person doing the yelling is the dope, not the crew who are being yelled at. So keep that in mind the next time you want to yell.

There is a sailing club in my area that loves to tell stories of their members' mishaps. When the members do silly things like going aground or dragging anchor, the club gives them little pennant flags that depict the mistake they made. A picture of a dragon pulling an anchor represents dragging anchor. A piece of rope tied around a big toe means they had to be towed. Silly things like that. And if you were the rescuer, you would get a picture of a lollipop, for being the good ship lollipop.

I was at one of the club meetings and they proceeded to tell the story of a couple who dragged anchor three times in one weekend, needed to be towed three times, and on and on until by the time they finished the story this couple received something like sixteen flags. At the end of the year, the club gives a special flag to the boat with the most flags. There is one word on it, "DUH."

I talked to the couple with the multiple flags and the guy told me, as if it were a badge of honor, *"I'm a self-taught sailor."* Hello! It seems he missed a few chapters in the sailing manual! What is up with that? Come on, this is not something to brag about. Those pennants are a polite pluck in the head. They are letting you know you're missing

something. There are obviously some gaps in your knowledge. And where there are gaps, there usually is a lot of yelling.

When it comes to knowing what you are doing on the big blue sea, I have a few strong beliefs. First, don't mess with Mother Nature. She is not to be tempted because she can be unpredictable, like most women, and you are neither big enough nor bad enough to take her on. I am very humble on the water. Second, ego and arrogance can get you killed. Third, if you are not learning, you are dying.

With everything in life, the process of growth is exemplified in a plant. The moment something stops growing it starts dying. So I am always looking for ways I can grow, learn, and improve my skills and knowledge. I am nowhere near perfect, and expect I never will be. I'm not in the same league with Peter Isler or any of those America Cup or Volvo Ocean Racers, and really have no desire to be. Can I improve? Absolutely!

When you think you know it all, you have probably only scratched the surface. There is always room for improvement. There is much less yelling when there is more humility.

YELLING *AT* IS INAPPROPRIATE

Profanity or derogatory comments are never acceptable. It is never okay to yell at someone, insult him, or call him inappropriate names. It is never acceptable to belittle someone or make him feel stupid, particularly when he is learning. By now, you know my philosophy: K.I.S.S., or Keep It Simple Sweetheart. It is about helping those who are less experienced. A novice is not stupid when he has never been taught the right words or the right way of doing things. I don't think that it is ever acceptable to make disparaging remarks when speaking to anyone on a boat, no matter what their skill level. I don't tolerate it on or off the boat.

Many men have told me that they do not care to be yelled at or insulted any more than women do. If the helmsman cannot convey his or her request in an appropriate way, then that is the person to whom those comments should be applied. We've all heard that when you point a finger at someone else, there are three of them pointing back at you. Shame on anyone who feels that insults are an appropriate motivator.

Too often, people just want to get out on the water and they compromise by sailing with Captain Bligh. I say to Captain Bligh: you are what you speak. So think about it next time you open your mouth. Are you telling everyone that you are really the idiot? You are the one who was supposed to convey the correct information when giving instructions. If your crew didn't understand you,then you are to blame.

New studies show that when a person gets angry, their IQ drops. When you are angry and upset, you don't think clearly, so it only makes matters worse. If you don't like the way people are doing things, do them yourself, but don't think that watching you do everything will somehow magically teach them the correct way. Demonstration is only a part of teaching.

I often have professional educators and professors in my sailing classes, and I have received a lot of great feedback and ideas from them. Here is some advice from the experts: If you are repeating yourself and the person is not responding to the directions you gave him, then it means that what you are saying does not compute. You should change your wording so he can better comprehend what you are asking. It is not the student or crew that must adapt. It is the person giving directions who must better clarify what it is that they want. Simply rewording your request can make all the difference in the world for a person who is struggling.

There is always more than one way of saying something. We have a variety of personalities, learning styles and ways to understand things, so we must use various ways to convey information to others. For instance, a student was doing a jibe. She needed to sheet the main in first, and then take the wraps off the winch and allow the mainsail to blow to the other side. I kept saying to her, "Release it." When she didn't let go of the line, I finally changed my words to, "Take the wraps off the winch and let the mainsail go back out." She finally understood and everything was great. She just didn't understand what I meant when I said, "Release it," so she kept pulling the sheet instead. Raising my voice was not going to make her comprehend the information any better.

We build our confidence through a succession of small accomplishments. These compound, sometimes without our realizing it, until we suddenly feel confident in our skills and abilities. This can work in the opposite direction as well. If we do something incorrectly and don't understand the reason why it is not working, we will keep making the same mistake. Eventually we will quit trying because we don't want to repeatedly fail. Repeated failures may translate to a false belief that one is a failure.

YELLING *TO* IS APPROPRIATE

If you take the time to discuss anticipated situations, such as docking, you can often be prepared and not have the need to yell at anyone. I know that even with the best-laid plans there are still times when yelling is necessary, so let's explore those reasons why we might yell.

When is it time to yell? We first need to clarify: talking loudly or shouting to be heard is not yelling. The word "yell" is a four-letter word that has a negative connotation. Often yelling comes with criticism or the insinuation that someone is stupid. There is a difference between being stupid—knowing what is correct and not doing it—and being ignorant, which is not knowing what is correct. You can't hold ignorance against a person who is in a learning environment. That is why he is there in the first place!

We may need to change the verb, because the word "yell" has collected so many negative connotations over the years. As you will see, there are many times when we need to raise our voices to be heard. This is a very important safety consideration. If we are using two-way communication and avoiding assumptions, we will understand that the person yelling at us, or raising his voice, is doing so to be heard, not to insult. Distinguishing yell AT from yell TO should take care of all the negative associations. Here are some valid reasons why we might yell TO someone.

1. TO BE HEARD, WHEN YOU CAN'T SEE EACH OTHER

When on deck or when you can't make eye contact, you do not know if you are heard without a response. So talking louder is a way to get an answer acknowledging that you were heard. A good example is someone on deck bringing the main sail down. On my boat there is a bimini that prevents the crew and helmsman from seeing each other. The crew may need to call to the helmsman because he is not keeping the boat into the wind, or the crew needs assistance with easing the halyard. The crew is calling to the helmsman, "Turn the boat into the wind." It's obvious that he did not hear because the boat is not turning and there is no verbal response. So now the crew must repeat the request. If he still does not get an answer, he must increase the volume to be heard and to get a response.

There are no insults involved, no derogatory comments, just a need to be heard and to receive an acknowledgement.

What if it were the helmsman telling the crew to hang on because there is a big wake coming? Is that yelling in a negative way? No, it's making sure people are holding on and staying safe. Giving an answer assures the helmsman and anyone below decks that they won't have to worry about doing an M.O.B. drill.

People are usually timid when learning initially and I will have to coach them to raise their voices to be heard. It only takes one problem to occur to make everyone realize the importance of being heard and getting a response.

2. TO BE HEARD OVER THE WIND

If the crew is at the bow they will have to raise their voice to be heard by the helmsman, and it will have to be even louder if there is a lot of wind.

We dragged our anchor at Longboat Key in Bradenton, Florida and of course, it was a dark and stormy night. When the wind picked up, we found ourselves not only on the lee shore but also drifting toward it quickly.

The boats had swung around so that we were headed right for the stern of a powerboat as we pulled our anchor up. The wind was blowing so hard that I could not hear my student, who was pulling up the anchor at the bow. I had his wife at the middle of the boat by the shrouds, conveying the information between us. It could have been disastrous had we not had a way to hear each other.

All I could see was that we were headed straight for the stern of the other boat and had no idea how much further we would have to go to retrieve the anchor. Finally, just in the nick of time, I heard him shout something and she yelled to me, "The anchor is up." I turned the helm hard over to steer away from the other boat and take us around to a new place to drop anchor.

It would have been impossible for us to hear each other had we not had that third person to relay the information back and forth between us. With all the wind he was shouting to her and she was shouting to me. There was a whole lot of shouting going on. But I don't think that anyone felt like they were being yelled AT!

Also, it's important to note that handheld radios would not have worked in this situation because he needed both hands to pull up the anchor. If you do opt for electronics over shouting, make sure the headsets or radios are waterproof!

3. TO GET SOMEONE'S ATTENTION

If you have done any sailing or boating at all you know there are times when people are just not paying attention. You may need to be heard by people on other boats.

The worst situations are when you are coming or going out of a marina. You might have a fuel dock and a boat ramp right next to each other. Inevitably there will be boats leaving the boat ramp and the person at the helm does not even bother to look behind him as they come blasting out of the ramp in reverse. Of course, if you have your horn near the helm (as you should), you can give them a blast. Technically it is five blasts for danger or doubt, but most of the time you just need one blast to get their attention. Part of the crew's job as the lookout is to shout to the other boat, "Hey look out!" when there might be a potentially dangerous situation, if nothing else, then to alert the helmsman to the problem. Both cases would require some shouting to make sure you are heard the first time.

Are you beginning to see the pragmatic difference between getting yelled AT and getting yelled TO? When you raise your voice, it's usually because you are not getting an answer so your only assumption can be that you were not heard. This is not a mean or hurtful thing that should cause a fight; it should be a reason to kiss that person and thank them for caring and keeping you safe.

4. IN M.O.B. OR EMERGENCY SITUATIONS

Of course there needs to be a balance when it comes to the number of people communicating, more so than ever when there is a victim in the water. On a bigger boat you may need several people relaying information, but not so many people talking that it causes distraction or confusion for the helmsman.

Too many people talking could cause a misinterpretation. So it should be agreed that only the person designated as the spotter and the helmsman will speak to each other. Yelling is allowed–whatever it takes to be heard and to recover the victim as quickly as possible. The person who is the spotter should never stop pointing, or stop talking to the helmsman until the helmsman can see the victim in front of the boat, or until the victim is back on the boat.

You will use a combination of both verbal and non-verbal communication to get that victim safely back on the boat. This is where the rubber meets the road and your communication skills are really put to the test.

5. WHEN YOU ARE NOT GETTING A RESPONSE

If you are verbally communicating with someone who is far away, like calling from the bow, there are two choices: repeat yourself until you get a response, or make the assumption you were heard and accept the consequences. It is usually the woman looking for a response from a cave dweller. A quick, "Okay," really goes a long way for her.

When two people (i.e. a couple) are sailing together, it means they are sailing short-handed. It means not having the luxury of extra crew to assist. A couple must rely on each other and leave nothing open to misinterpretation. Again, a verbal acknowledgement assures the other person that he has been heard and understood. If they have extra crew, they might place a person amidships at the shrouds to relay information between helmsman and the person at the bow. This becomes increasingly important on boats over forty feet.

The couple on the front cover of this book, Ricardo and Julie, told me an amusing story. I arrived at the boat one morning and Julie said something to the effect of, "Josie, you have changed my marriage!" She explained that Ricardo was walking to the parking lot to get something out of their car when she shouted, "Do you have your keys?" He was never good at giving a verbal response prior to the class and normally he would not bother to respond to her. But this time was different. Although he did not miss a stride or turn around and look at her, he did put his hand up in the air, showing her that he had the keys, and shouted back, "Got it!"

6. TO SHOW URGENCY

I can give many instances when urgency can cause someone to raise his voice. I say this in defense of the guys who appear to be shouting out commands to the wife. He is responding to a situation. He doesn't always know exactly what to do, nor does he know if what he is asking is going to work or not. He will continue to change the game plan until something works. This is not personal and is in no way meant to leave her out of the picture. He is just a guy reacting and responding to the problem in the way guys do.

131

We don't always have the time to give each other detailed explanations. We just need to keep trying things until something works. The response to crisis is that gender difference that makes women tend to do nothing while guys tend to try anything. This is usually the worst thing for a woman because she feels she is being yelled at and not being given enough information. Ladies, you just have to realize that sometimes someone sees something that you have missed. He is reacting and responding. It is nothing personal, although it may feel like it at the time.

Women need to know the reason why. They are looking for explanations. In some cases there just isn't time to give those explanations without causing dire consequences, so you will have to trust the process. A follow-up discussion really goes a long way towards assuring people that they didn't do anything wrong, it was just about dealing with the situation and also, that there just wasn't time to tell the whole story at the time of the crisis.

Demanding an explanation, or arguing over how to do something can cause a minor problem to become a major problem. In a situation like this there should be the designated captain who steps up, and the person in the crew position who takes the back seat for the moment. When you talk about what happened after the fact, you will gain new insights and understanding, which will give you both more confidence to handle things better the next time.

Examples of conflict-causing crises exist in a multitude of docking situations. What can go wrong with this? Let me count the ways. The boat is being blown onto the neighbor's boat. The boat is hitting the dock box. The boat is hitting the piling. (Should I continue?) The current is causing the boat to go into the slip sideways and to throttle up would mean hitting something. Yikes! We will talk more about these situations in the chapter on docking and anchoring.

A good example with the roles reversed happened when I had a husband at the helm for an M.O.B. practice drill. While he was trying to do a figure-eight maneuver, he missed the cushion the first pass so we had to try again. He had already eased the main sheet all the way out, and I was now trying to get sails back under control to make another pass. When he made his second attempt to retrieve the victim, he started to jibe rather than tack. This caused the jib to wrap the wrong way around the headstay. Then, because the main sheet had already been eased too much, it was now caught on the traveler. I quickly told him, "Head up." I grabbed the jib sheet and quickly pulled the jib back behind the headstay. I immediately told him, "Head down," so I could release the main sheet from where it was caught on the traveler.

He started yelling at me, "I don't know what you want!" Boy, was that a flash back! I really did not have time to give him an explanation of all the things that I was seeing. I was reacting and responding to the situation as I saw it. Again, no time to explain, I was just hoping that it wouldn't become worse than it already was. At the same time I shouted out to his wife on the bow, "Get down and hold on." I wanted her to hear me the first time. My concern was that the jib sheets were whipping wildly and could injure her, or worse, knock her off the boat and we would have a real M.O.B. situation. Again, no time to explain.

He yelled at me because he felt out of control and didn't understand everything that was happening. Once the boat was back under control I calmly explained everything to both of them. When things started going wrong, it was not that either one of them had done anything wrong, it was just urgent that I respond to the situation and give instructions to get things back under control as quickly as possible. The real problem would have occurred had I taken the time to try and explain what was happening to either of them—what I was seeing and why I wanted them to do one thing or another. I was using the masculine approach – respond first, explain later. Sometimes the words just don't come out. There is only time to react to the situation in order to minimize the damage or danger.

These situations can be very scary at the time and that feeling of not being in control causes anxiety, which we already know comes out differently in men and women. Feelings get hurt, misunderstandings take place and then everyone is upset with each other. Stop it! Talk about it. After a crisis, it should be routine to discuss the situation. Get a clear understanding of everything that took place, and help each other see the other's perspective. Know that both of you share the goal of keeping the boat safe and under control. Now you will be better prepared for the next time and you don't have to blame each other. This is positive growth.

7. TO SHOW EXCITEMENT & HAPPINESS

Of course, there are some times when life is just so good out there; the seas are perfect, the wind is warm, and we see dolphins or whales and we cannot contain ourselves. We simply must shout for joy. Wahoo!

CB

As my mother always told me, if you can't say anything nice don't say anything at all. It's a good policy. It's related to the golden rule, which helps too—treat others the way you want to be treated. Always try to find the lesson in a situation-gone-wrong. Ask, how can we improve ourselves as individuals and team-members? How could I have responded better? How do I want to respond next time the situation arises? If you do yell at someone, don't be afraid to apologize. An apology can mend where an excuse can cause resentment. "I'm sorry" if it is genuinely spoken can plug a leak in a relationship and help keep it afloat.

NINE

The Steps to Go from Living on Land to Living Aboard

I ended up buying my boat five years, almost to the day, after I had declared that I would do it. I amazed even myself.

Most women cannot go from zero to sixty in three seconds. Guys, don't take a woman on a boat for the first time and think she will instantly share the dream of sailing around the world with you. Does this story sound familiar? He has been dreaming about it all of his life and she is either just learning about this life-long fantasy or is reluctantly going along with it.

My boyfriend wanted me to buy into the idea of getting a boat, living aboard and sailing to Tahiti. I thought he was nuts. Oddly enough, ten years later, it was I who bought the boat, lived aboard and sailed to Tahiti. Go figure!

Most people do not adapt to drastic changes. What usually happens—and this is related to the man being a cave dweller—is that he has been thinking, dreaming and reading about sailing the seven seas, maybe all of his life, but he may or may not have expressed his real desires to his wife completely. His dream got put on the back burner as he pursued things like family and career. Oh, he may have thrown out little tidbits, from time to time, but she didn't take him seriously, until now. The kids are grown and gone, and he wants to sell the house and go sailing.

For most people, life usually overshadows the dreams of their youth, and things like college, marriage, building the career, and raising children take the spotlight. Now that the kids are finishing college, he is bringing up this sailing thing again, twenty or thirty years later. She is hoping it is just a mid-life crisis that will go away. The house is almost paid for, and decorated just the way she has always wanted it. Life is easier now that the kids are raised and she is ready to relax. To her, he is bringing up this dream of sailing around the world out of the blue. It comes as a surprise and she may meet it with a lot of opposition. She views this as losing all of her comforts and her security. She doesn't see this as an adventure but more as a nightmare. She imagines the worst, thinking he will get hurt and she will not know what to do, or worse, they could both end up dying.

I remember my father bringing this up to my mother. She said, "What am I supposed to do if you die out there?" He told her, "Well, just cut my thumb off and keep it for proof and then just throw my body overboard." I can still hear the terror in her voice, "Great, then they will arrest me for murder. And how will I prove I didn't kill you?" He would laugh.

My mother always worried that Dad would try to get her onto a boat. She didn't even swim. This was about the worst thing he could ask of her. She spent fifty years following him around the world with his military career, being uprooted every three or four years. What about all the sacrifices she had made for him? After he retired, she finally got her stable home in Florida, where she still lives today. The sad thing is that my father never got to live his dream.

When Jack started suggesting to me the idea of buying a boat and living aboard, he would show me different styles and sizes of boats all the time. He really tried hard to get me engaged in his dream, and what seemed to me a crazy lifestyle. I was not at all into it. I couldn't visualize myself on these tiny cracker-box boats, even the forty-four-foot Peterson, which had a center cockpit, large aft cabin and private head. It was all teak and beautiful, I will admit. But there was no way I could imagine living full-time on something that small! I lived in a house that was over 2500 square feet with three bedrooms; living in this tiny space was insanity to me. At that point, I didn't love sailing enough to even imagine what Jack wanted to do. I was okay going out on the boat for day-sails and weekend trips and even the week-long trips sailing in the Pacific Northwest. But living full-time in that confined space was the furthest thing from my mind.

After all the objections I had, the funny thing was that I ended up living aboard my twenty-eight-foot O'day for seven years. Can you even imagine? Well, changing my mind was a process and it didn't happen over night. Never say never.

THE PROCESS

A woman needs to fall in love with sailing, just like she did with the man in her life. Then, if she's turned on to the dream, it's important for a couple to take one step at a time as they shift from one lifestyle to the other. It's so much easier to downsize in small steps. In general, small changes are easier to make than big ones. And don't forget that learning to sail is as important a step as any other part of this process!

1. FALL IN LOVE

The first thing I discovered was that I had fallen in love with sailing. Then I could begin to think about scaling down step by step. I really had to buy into that whole dream of cruising, traveling and imagining where this little boat could take me before I could even do that. It took a few years. It was definitely not overnight. So how does it happen? This is how it worked for me.

First, I started falling in love with sailing and all the things that sailing on a boat offered. To me it was being surrounded by nature and feeling a sense of freedom. I loved the idea of traveling by water, and I loved meeting people and hearing the stories that other people would tell of their own travels and adventures.

Our second trip up the inside passage to Desolation Sound hooked

me. I was so amazed at the places we went, and how few other people we saw out on the water. Yet there was a real connection to the few people that we did meet. I love waterfalls and to anchor near a seventy foot waterfall was about as good as it gets in my opinion. There was one night when Jack and I met these other people in the anchorage who had gotten some large prawns from some fishermen. Jack invited them over for dinner. He made pasta, I made fresh bread and they brought the prawns. We had a party on the boat and everyone told stories.

I remember back when Jack and I had only been dating for about a year. One day he called me up and out of the blue, he told me that he had put a $1,000 deposit on a boat and one of us needed to give up our apartments so we could afford the boat. I freaked out. I told him I didn't even know his financial situation and that he was moving way too fast for me. I told him to come over and we could talk about this. He took me down to the boat and showed it to me. It was a race boat of course.

He explained to me how he would rip this section of the boat out and move the galley from one side to the other and change this and do that. I said, "Why don't you just build yourself a boat so that it is exactly like you want it in the first place?" I couldn't understand why he wouldn't just buy the boat the way he wanted it in the first place.

Next, we sat down and discussed both of our finances. It was the first time I even knew how much money he made. This was just too overwhelming for me. I couldn't imagine how we were going to pull this off. We talked about it and then slept on it. In the end, I told him to get his deposit back, because it was just more than I was ready for, which he did.

The following year Jack and I took several weeks and sailed a different boat from Gig Harbor, Washington, up through Seattle to Desolation Sound via Vancouver, British Columbia. We had picked up another friend in Vancouver, Randy, and Randy's wife drove up to Lund to meet us the next day. We spent a week with them and then another two weeks sailing back to Seattle via the San Juan Islands. It was on this trip that I truly fell in love with sailing.

I can't tell you what it was that hooked me. I think it was an

accumulation of things: the serenity of being in nature—the woods, the mountains, and the peaceful water. I loved where boats could take me, and the idea of being able to travel with all your belongings. You don't have to pack. I had always wanted to travel and this seemed like a great way to see the world. I also loved the people we met and the stories I heard. It seemed like a world of which I didn't think I could ever afford to be a part, but here I was immersed in it, and I could visualize my future. I thought, "Some day, I will have my own stories to tell."

The only problem was that now things weren't going so great between us, so when Jack asked what I thought about this whole idea of buying a boat and living aboard my response was, "I want to buy a boat, but not with you." I didn't say it in a mean way. I was just being honest. I had too many girlfriends who had boat partners. Neither one was willing to give up their half of the boat when the relationship didn't work out.

It was like something clicked in me from that trip and from then on I was on a mission to find a way to buy my own boat. It seems a little crazy now that I think about it. I didn't even own my own home yet, but here I was looking for a boat. Crazy, huh?

I ended up moving out of my three-bedroom house into a one-bedroom apartment. I remember vividly starting to hyperventilate when I looked at the small one-bedroom apartments. How could I possibly fit into that tiny space? Once I got settled into my little six-hundred–square-foot place, I adapted.

Now, I got my break because my brother had a thirty-eight-foot Downeast in Miami, Florida; I was able to do a trial period before making the commitment of purchasing a boat of my own. *Try it before you buy it*, right? I spent three months living on the boat and never felt claustrophobic or confined at all. It was a great experience, and at the end of the three months, with lots of excursions on Biscayne Bay and down to the Keys, I was ready for a trip to Bimini in the Bahamas.

We had the perfect overnight passage with about ten knots of breeze and requiring only one tack all night. What more could you ask for? As we were cruising around the islands, I would stand at the bow and call back to my brother, "How deep is it?" He would say, "ten feet." I would call in amazement, "I can see the bottom." A little while later I shouted out the same question. Now he said, "thirty feet." I was shocked, "I can still see the bottom!" He was just laughing. I can't remember how deep it was when I vowed right then and there, that if I was going to buy a boat and live on it, I wanted to do it in Florida because of the warm weather and proximity to such great cruising grounds.

Now imagine how much stuff you can fit into the trunk of a Mazda Miata. That's the car in which I drove to Florida and that's how much stuff I took with me. I learned that most of the stuff I had, I didn't miss while I was living on the boat in Florida, so it wasn't hard to part with.

When I went to Florida, my sailing friends were sure I was not going to come back to Washington. I kept telling them, "I love the Pacific Northwest. I can't imagine living anywhere else." My famous last words! I drove back to Seattle, sold everything I owned, and packed up what was left; three months later I was back in Florida. That's what happens when you're in love.

2. DOWNSIZE AND SIMPLIFY

Now you have to realize that part of what made this process possible was that I had given up all of my worldly possessions for three months while living on my brother's boat. I thought about this and couldn't think of anything that I really missed. Stuff is stuff and anything that you really feel you cannot give up, I suggest you put in storage, like all good live-aboards do. It's true; most live-aboards have either passive or active storage. Passive means renting a storage unit, active is putting your furniture or belongings in the care of a trusted friend or relative for safekeeping.

Keep in mind that it has to be done in phases. When I first moved to Florida I rented a furnished studio apartment. Again, I brought very little stuff with me from Seattle. So this made it easier.

Simplify and reduce your material burden. If you want to cruise someday, but you're not quite ready yet, what steps can you take to

prepare yourselves for that future? Do you really need two vehicles? How about moving into a smaller place? If you're actively looking for a boat to live aboard, look at your belongings. What are the basic necessities? What personal or luxury items can you simply not live without? Which special keepsakes will you pack up, and which will you give away as mementos to good friends? These are some of the things you will think through as you take this step.

3. PRACTICE

Some husbands, even with the best of intentions, will do all the wrong things from the get-go. A recent student of mine bought a little boat and the first time he took his wife out on it, he scared her senseless. He had obviously been talking about buying a bigger boat and living aboard, because the first thing she told me was, "I'm not selling my house."

While it may seem like an off-the-wall comment, I have heard and seen these patterns frequently enough that I understand the dynamics of the process. Whenever I would ask her how she was doing, she would tell me, "I'm not going to admit to liking anything, because if I do, my husband is going to go buy a boat tomorrow." She obviously was not ready to make the big change that he was dying to make.

I finally made the two of them come to an agreement that he would not show her any boats until the end of the summer so she could just get out there and have fun without the pressure of having her entire life altered. Once we took that weight off of her shoulders she finally started having fun. As we were coming down the channel to the slip our last day of classes she hollered from the bow of the boat to her husband, "We are naming the boat *Not Too Old Yet*." I always know that when the wife decides on a name for the boat, she has fallen in love and is ready to begin the process.

This story emphasizes the need to spend time out on the water having a good time before you buy a boat. If you start out as confident sailors, the stress of learning to sail your boat will be less than if you are new to both the boat and to sailing. Get lessons, either individually or as a couple. This does not necessarily mean you need certifications. It does mean you need some time at the helm of a boat; practice makes perfect.

4. PRIORITIZE

So, first you need to like to sail and then to learn to sail, and then you can decide what is important to you. Do you want to sell everything? Do you want to live full-time or part-time onboard? Do you want to cruise part-time or full-time? Where do you want to go and what will it take to get there? Can you buy the boat and still get a little condo so that you aren't giving up the land-life completely? At what level are you willing to commit? Do you want one foot on the boat and one on land? You shouldn't have to give it all up; some people keep their houses, and others scale down. Some plan to fly home to family a few times a year no matter where they are. Others rent their houses out when they leave.

Living aboard part-time, seasonally, for instance, is a great way to start making the transition. I met one couple recently who have been sailing like that for the last five years. They rent their house out for six months and the rent money finances their cruising. They have all their personal and private belongings locked in one room and it takes them only a couple of days to make the house theirs again once they return.

Can you live with putting your things in storage? When it is time to scale down? What do you give up and what do you keep? Make a list of what is important to you. Decide what you absolutely will not give up, what you are willing to totally give up and what are you willing to compromise on. The list will change over time. Remember, don't be too rigid. Things that don't bend will break, while things that are flexible bounce back.

Keep those things that are important to you on the boat. Things like certain dishes, linens, blankets and clothing. The less you feel like you are giving up or giving in, the less it will feel like you are surrendering and more that you are embarking on a new chapter of your life. And remember, you can always go back. Nothing is set in stone except what is engraved on your headstone. You can add, change, reevaluate and try different things until you find what works for both of you.

I can tell you, there have been many times, especially on a bad day, when I have declared that I am done with this whole sailing thing. You know, one of those days where too many things have gone wrong all at once, or, worse, a bad weather day? But once the sun comes out and the breezes are light and warm again, I think, 'I can't imagine doing anything else.'

5. BUY A BOAT

I ended up buying my boat five years, almost to the day, after I had declared to Jack that I would do it. I amazed even myself. Yet another reason for her name -*Tididi*.

The biggest fear for me was the engine. It held me back for a long time because I really don't have much in the way of mechanical ability. Engines intimidated me. I really wanted a boat thirty to thirty-six feet long, but with minimal financial resources, I wasn't even sure what I was going to do with it once I got it. I couldn't make up my mind about living aboard a boat as small as *Tididi*.

In the end, it was the amenities that sold me on this boat. She had a hot water tank, a real refrigerator—not just an icebox, roller furling, a bimini and dodger, autopilot and radar. Yes, radar on a twenty-eight-foot boat! Not only that, but the selling feature was that she had just been repowered with a brand new Yanmar. That was the real reason why I bought this little boat. It was perfect for my first boat, and learning how to single-hand her was achievable, in my mind.

I didn't think I would live on a boat that small, but from the day I bought her and moved her into her new slip, I started moving aboard. Within a couple of months I moved out of my apartment. Fifteen months after I bought her, I was off, cruising the Bahamas.

I really took to heart what Lin and Larry Pardy say, "Go small, go simple and go now." I really believe that. Life is short. You can live your life making dreams come true with lots of memories, or you can live with regret and *what if's*. I wanted to make those dreams a reality.

The process of buying a boat is scary for everyone. You have to understand that there are different types of boats for different goals. Are you coastal cruising, planning ocean passages, or just day-sailing on the lake? Do you want a monohull or multihull? So not only what kind of boat, but how big of a boat do you want? Can you afford it? You also have to figure out where you will keep the boat and add the dockage to the cost of having a boat. There are a lot of things to ponder. And just as you go through "buyer's remorse" with purchasing a car or a home, you can go through the whole gamut of emotions with a boat purchase.

Buying a boat is even more intimidating as a single woman. Most women will never enjoy the pleasure of owning a boat, because they allow all the fears and *what if's* to prevent them from accomplishing their dreams. As it was for me, the biggest fear for single women is usually related to the engine. However, more and more single women are going for it, and finding that things work out for them, as they did for me. There are always people around the docks, and even out cruising, to help if you should need it. Sometimes it's an opportunity to meet someone new, which can be fun.

Gregg Nestor wrote a book entitled, *Twenty Affordable Sailboats to Take You Anywhere*. He demonstrates that anyone can find a boat that suits his own needs and pocketbook. It doesn't have to be a brand new boat. I want to encourage all women, married or single, to go for it! It isn't always easy, but nothing is more rewarding than working through all the challenges. Don't get me wrong, there have been many hard times when I have wanted to sell this boat and give up on the whole idea. However, my confidence came from surviving those same hard times.

6. GET PREPARED

Buying a boat and living aboard had been my obsession for five years, after the three-week cruise in Desolation Sound. My experience of cruising for those three weeks changed my life so much that I was willing to leave my home of twenty years, in Seattle, to go all the way to

Florida and pursue finding my home on the water. I fulfilled this dream with Tididi in 1998, but I still had fears.

My obsession with living aboard and cruising took over my "sense of responsibility," according to my friends. They thought that as a single female, and a blonde, I would get myself into trouble. I thought I was tough enough. I live by the Nike rule, *life's short, play hard.* I knew I couldn't do it all and I also knew that there were a lot of scary things out there, but I was willing to step out into the unknown despite my uncertainties.

What I didn't expect when I bought my boat was how it increased my desire to go cruising and traveling afar. My home was now this twenty-eight-foot O'day. How would I get this boat prepared, since I knew nothing about electrical systems, motors or rigging? How could I go out there as a single woman and not worry about having men make unwanted advances? *What if...what if...what if...*

Recently, I was at the Annapolis Boat Show when I ran into the first couple who ever took classes from me. They were looking for a boat, and they were having an argument over which equipment was a necessity and which was a luxury. When the wife came to me, thinking that I would take her side about not needing the radar, she was shocked when I said I agreed with her husband. It can mean peace of mind, and that is worth the money.

Don't think you need all the bells and whistles to go cruising, but if it's safety-related, it's a must. Besides, if you get out there and find you need to come back to do more work, you can always call it your shake down cruise. Everyone knows that cruising is just taking your boat to exotic locations to work on it.

7. JUST GO

Set a date and follow your dreams. As they say, "There are those who talk about it and then those who just do it. Which one will you be?

Note: For further reading on this topic see the last chapter on Women's Resources.

Two on a Boat How to Keep it Afloat

TEN

THE FOUNDATION OF SAILING IS UNDERSTANDING THE WIND

The foundation of sailing is about understanding the wind When you don't get this you don't get anything on a boat. Learning to sail should be simple and fun!

"Head up." That one phrase caused me so much apprehension that eventually I cringed at being asked to take the helm. It was no longer fun for me. It was not only a source of frustration, but also fear. I dreaded seeing that look of disgust and annoyance on my boyfriend's face when I did the wrong thing. I was so sure that I was going to do the wrong thing that it became a self-fulfilling prophecy. I would inevitably turn the wrong way, especially on a boat with a tiller.

I did okay if he wasn't paying attention or if I sailed with someone else who didn't care, but he was a *racer* and expected perfection and speed, neither of which I could ever achieve under his watchful eye.

Learning to sail is not rocket science, even though some people would like you to think so. You can go as shallow or as deep as you'd like into the subjects of physics, aerodynamics and naval architecture, but if you can't understand the basics—how the wind works and affects your boat; that knowledge is pretty much worthless. You can't control a boat effectively on theory alone.

I have watched so many women struggle to the point of tears while trying to grasp this invisible monster. I can relate to those women because of my own experiences with not understanding the wind and having a sailing partner who, although he was great at handling a boat, could never give me any kind of explanation to help me understand the basic aspects of sailing. Doing what I was told did not help me to learn.

I can't tell you how often I have heard women boaters and cruisers tell me the same thing. "I just do what I am told." Nothing breaks my heart more than when I hear that statement. She does what she is told because she really doesn't have a clue. I know there isn't a woman alive who cannot learn the wind once the information is presented to her in the way she is wired to learn. The basics of sailing are so simple, but the problem is that every training manual on the market is designed and written in the way men are wired to learn, not women. I will say it again; it's not bad, it's just different!

Remember, women are visual and relational, not linear and logical. So having a woman read a sailing book with diagrams showing several boats on different points of sail and asking her to distinguish one from another is like asking someone who is color blind to distinguish between the colors of red and green. She sees the boats, but she can't conceptualize how their positions relate to the wind, or how one would adjust the sails. How does one get from diagram A to diagram B? They just *can't SEE IT!*

Even out on the water, men and women perceive the wind differently. She thinks of the wind in relation to herself, while he thinks of it in relation to the boat. The guy says, "Don't you see the wind up on the bow?" and she feels like crying because she just cannot see what he is talking about. He can't see it either, since wind is invisible, but he is able to interpret the cues given by the wind and see how it affects the boat. She deals with things relationally, so she needs to feel the wind

HIS WAY vs. HER WAY

His View When Learning Points-of-Sail
He sees the wind in relationship to the boat

Her View When Learning Points-of-Sail
She sees the wind in relationship to herself

and know how it will affect her. She also has a much harder time because she needs a bigger picture. A detail like, "the wind shifted ten degrees" is meaningless to her. In reality, neither is right or wrong, and often once each person grasps how the other sees it, they can appreciate both views. It's like a visual puzzle that has a picture within a picture. You may not see the second picture at first glance, but once you know it is there, you are able to see them both.

It is the thrill of watching the light come on that made it a delight for me to teach sailing. People get so excited once they see how simple sailing really is. They quickly gain confidence, especially if they can learn to feel and visualize the wind instead of using that wind vane at the top of the mast. (I call it a "pain in the neck" because if you keep looking up at it long enough, that's exactly what you'll get.) Everything becomes easy after that. It is the foundation of everything on a sailboat. A house cannot stand if the foundation is shaky, but if the foundation is solid, everything can be built up from there.

After teaching these concepts to couples and women over the years, I finally realized what was missing. I would get students who would tell me they already knew how to sail. I would ask them, "Do you know your points of sail?" and they would answer that they did. But when I took them out on the water and asked them to put the boat on a beam reach, for example, they wouldn't know which way to turn boat. Should they go up or down? Knowing the names of the points of sail does not tell you how to orient the boat to the wind. It doesn't tell you whether to execute a tack or a jibe. I had been asking the wrong questions. The questions should be: *Do you understand the wind? Do you know which way is up? What is the difference between tacking and jibing? Do you know how and where to turn the boat when you get a shift in the wind?*

They say necessity is the mother of invention. I tried to find diagrams and other tools to help my students conceptualize the wind and learn how to respond to it. I used many techniques to help students "see" and feel the wind with only limited success. I knew my female students struggled to "get it," and the more I learned about gender differences, the more I realized that I would have to come up with a way to help women understand the wind. That's where the *Sailing Wind Wheel* comes in.

The *Sailing Wind Wheel* was developed to make learning to sail easy for the most reluctant beginner. I do not introduce it here to toot my own horn, although I am the creator. If someone else had thought of a way to teach women to sail the way they needed to be taught, I would be introducing their three-dimensional, interactive learning tool! As it is, my students experienced immediate success, with both women and men able to visualize the wind, understand how it relates to the boat, and how to adjust the sails accordingly.

Statistics published by Knowledge Industry Publications in 1998 showed that visual training aids increase a person's understanding 400,000 times faster than text alone and improved learning by 400%. This is an amazing statistic. Other statistics show that over 55% of the entire population is made up of visual learners, regardless of age or gender. Since the majority of women are visual learners, and women tend to see things relationally, the *Sailing Wind Wheel* has quickly become a magic tool, making them "instant naturals on the water" as my friend Captain Dave Renoll, owner of R&R Charters in Annapolis, has put it. Women who have struggled for years are having epiphanies and saying, "I can do this," because sailing finally makes sense.

At the Chicago Boat Show, a woman named Lynn came to both of my seminars, and kept telling me, "I know my points of sail, I just don't know what to do when the wind shifts on me." Lynn spent three days with me and this is what she said afterwards:

I have been singing your praises this summer and have spent a lot of the time on the water, so I apologize for my tardiness with this reply. I wanted to tell you about how much you have helped me since I took your class last March! After years of sailing, I now am fully aware of the principles behind it. After taking your class, I am at the helm 75% of the time and "I Get It". Before your class, I never wanted to take the helm because I didn't really understand what to do. Now, I know which way to turn the boat in various wind conditions and I know the reasons WHY the sheets have to be adjusted and I can even adjust them the right way!

Jonathan Banks, the Director of Sail America, took the *Sailing Wind Wheel* home to show his family. He said he put it on the table and his wife looked at it, but didn't pay much attention. Then his son picked it up and said, "This is cool." The son showed his mother how it worked and she exclaimed that she finally understood the wind . She thought the *Sailing Wind Wheel* was brilliant, and wondered why it took so long for something like this to be created.

When Bob Bitchin's wife Jodie (owners of the magazine *Latitudes & Attitudes*), saw the *Sailing Wind Wheel* the first time, she told me she wished she had thought of it first. She totally got it. Why are all these women getting excited? Because the *Sailing Wind Wheel* is the first teaching tool that was designed in a way that makes sense, not only for women, but for anyone who is a visual learner.

This is what I have been seeing and hearing over and over again since I started using this teaching tool. Since every decision we make on a boat, from tacking, to approaching a dock, to retrieving something (or someone) that has fallen overboard, is dependant on understanding the wind, an interactive model that allows students to practice ahead of time will help them make better decisions on the water. Instructors instantly recognize the value of the *Sailing Wind Wheel*. Even their female students, who typically have difficulties at first, understand the basic concepts the first time around. Now many sailing schools and trainers are using the *Sailing Wind Wheel* around the US and in over fourteen other countries.

The beauty of the *Sailing Wind Wheel* is that sailors can use this tool on their boat and guide anyone on the basics of sailing with only a few minutes of explanation. Even if you are a racer, you can get your new crew up to speed very quickly before the start of the race.

After using the *Sailing Wind Wheel* at seminars and boat shows, I needed a concise way to present the basics of sailing. I always joke in class or in a seminar, "I don't know why everyone has such a difficult time learning to sail; there are only two of everything. Two sides of the boat, two sides to the wind, two directions to turn. Two – two – two. You always have a 50/50 chance of getting it right. What great odds!"

I put together a presentation and taught it to my next student, who happened to be a woman. She caught on instantly and told me that I was micro-teaching. I wasn't sure whether that was a good thing at first, but she explained that to break things down "microscopically" then build them back up again is an excellent method of teaching, and that's how the *2x2 Micro Method* manual was developed.

If you have not yet mastered the art of sailing then the *Sailing Wind Wheel* and *2x2 Micro Method* will make understanding the wind a breeze. You can teach yourself at home, or someone else in the cockpit of your boat in a very short period of time. If you are a beginner, I always suggest learning to feel the wind on land first, standing in front of a fan, on the dock, or at the beach. You can then use the *Sailing Wind Wheel* to practice turning the boat and adjusting the sails. When you can master the wind on shore with your eyes closed, you will never feel lost on the water again.

As helmsman, being able to announce your intentions to the other crew requires that you first need to know where the wind is, and then decide which way you're going to turn in relation to it. Every decision on a boat takes you back to the wind. Always make this your first question, "Where is the wind?" When you can answer this question, you will make good decisions and feel confident at the helm.

If you are interested in learning how to use this tool to your advantage, I now offer online training classes. You can go to www.womensailing.com to learn more about classes, books and seminars. If you haven't already purchased a *Sailing Wind Wheel*, here are some reasons why you need one on your boat.

 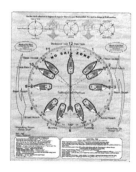

YOU NEED THE SAILING WIND WHEEL IF:

1. You have difficulty understanding the wind.
2. You want to learn to sail.
3. You know someone who is learning to sail.
4. You want to improve your sailing skills.
5. You are crew and want to improve your skills.
6. You are a guy trying to teach a girl.
7. You are in the process of taking sailing lessons.
8. You are a graduate of a sailing class and want a reminder.
9. You are a self-taught sailor.
10. You take guests aboard your boat and want an easy way to teach new crew.
11. You like to have all the latest on sailing for your library aboard or at home.
12. You are a professional sailing instructor and want to help your students learn quickly and easily.
13. Your sailing partner has never been able to help you understand the wind.
14. You want to teach your children.
15. You have sailing programs at your yacht club.
16.

(See the back of the book for ordering or just visit the sailingwindwheel.com web site)

Two on a Boat How to Keep it Afloat

ELEVEN

What to do When Things Go Wrong
and They Will

He said to me, "Don't you know what sh&*(^ happens when you are cruising?" I replied on the brink of tears, "No-o-o." He stated, "So that when you are in a bar telling stories, you are interesting!"

COMMON PROBLEMS AND HOW TO HANDLE THEM

"If adventures are created from faux pas and mishaps then my adventure has just begun!" That was the first line I wrote in my journal on December 4, 1999, the day we finally left Ft. Lauderdale. Imagine being in a twenty-eight-foot boat, seven miles off shore in over 1500 feet of water, and discovering that you are taking on water and the automatic bilge pump is not working. I went below to use the head and saw water gushing from the quarter berth, then found the bilge was already full of salt water!

With water gushing into the boat, Didier and I begin the frantic search for the monster attempting to take our life. I was holding the manual bilge switch, while he started removing the stores we had packed in our aft quarter berth. It didn't take long for me to start feeling queasy from being down below decks in five-foot seas. Talk about being tested! We finally discovered the culprit: a broken drain hose that ran from the cockpit scupper to the through-hull. The water kept gushing in because our through-hull was below the water line on our current tack.

That was just the first day out of Fort Lauderdale. The rest of the week out was similar to our first day, even though I had avoided a Friday departure. (All sailors know it's bad luck to start your trip on Friday!) Everything seemed to malfunction at once, we both felt sick, we ran aground, we had high winds at the most inopportune moments, and I could go on. If an experience like that doesn't make you put your tail between your legs and go back, you have won half the battle.

Tididi, as I've mentioned before, is "I did it" spelled backwards. It applies to the way I have done almost everything in my life, including my adventures. After I purchased in September of 1998, I became immediately infatuated with the idea of taking her cruising in the Caribbean. Even though I had only sailed in the waters of the Pacific Northwest, the Bahamas and Caribbean were a huge undertaking in my mind, as it meant crossing the Gulf Stream and being out of sight of land. Being a woman, I of course cannot explain my irrational fear of being capsized by a rogue wave, but suffice it to say that the anticipation and excitement I felt about cruising to the Caribbean was mixed with trepidation.

My learning curve was steep and my first experiences with cruising came with lots of lessons and challenges. When I up to my elbows in problems and things looked bleak, I would wonder how I got myself into this mess. Another single-hander, who was planning an around-the-world trip via the "roaring 40's", gave me his words of wisdom. He said, "Don't you know why sh**... happens?" With a quiver in my voice I replied, "No-o-o-o." He stated emphatically, "So that when you get home and you're telling stories in the bar, you're interesting!" Almost in tears I stated, "I don't want to be interesting!"

Good or bad, I found out that he was right. When I started teaching sailing, I realized that with almost every problem that we discussed in class, I was able to give a real life story to support it. I have a plethora of stories to tell about things-gone-wrong. And with almost every class I've taught, my students and I have added to the collection of stories. My students get to leave with their own tales to tell.

When I first started teaching sailing, I would get very upset when things didn't go as planned. But after all these years of sailing and

spending time on boats, it takes a lot to get me upset. When things go wrong, and they inevitably will, I just chalk it up to yet another story to tell.

The following list of *what ifs* is not comprehensive by any means, but whether you like to hear this or not, I will tell you that confidence comes from overcoming and learning from difficulties, mistakes and hardships. I've said it before, but I'll say it again: you don't know what you don't know! And that is what causes fear and stress in a new situation. Knowledge combats anxiety, which is why training is so important.

Please know this before you get started: *it's not a matter of if, it's a matter of when.* If you are not experiencing problems, that just means that you are not leaving the dock often enough. It is said that you are not really a sailor until you have a story about running aground. You might as well look forward to the experience instead of dreading it. Preparation and training eliminate a great deal of fear; so, know what to do *when* you run aground!

The important thing is to file the information in the back of your mind so that it's there when you need it. Talk to others who have experienced similar problems, so that you can learn something new or learn from their mistakes. I'm sure there are many of you who could help add to this list with your own stories. (Feel free to contribute your story for a future revision! Email your stories to sailing@sailingwindwheel.com.)

Some or most of these things are almost guaranteed to happen to you, if you sail long enough. If you think you that you are somehow immune to problems, you are going to be severely disappointed! Even if you only go out for a day-sail, you will run into some kind of a problem, sooner or later. It is always a shame when people don't see these mishaps as great opportunities to learn. Those are the people who usually make one passage and end up selling their boat and returning to land.

Keep in mind that there are entire books written on some of these topics. The more you experience, read and learn, the more information you will have to draw on when a situation arises. Now you are starting to know what you didn't know.

WHAT TO DO WHEN YOU RUN AGROUND

Notice that running aground is not a *what if*. There are two reasons why a sailor would say that he has never run ground. He is either lying about it or never leaves the dock. Without exception, every person I met while cruising had a story of running aground. You sit around having sunset drinks and everyone tries to top each other's grounding stories. So get out there and run aground so that you have a story to tell like the rest of us!

If you are not hard aground, meaning truly stuck, you can always sail or motor off of a shoal. The key is to ease the sheets and luff your sails quickly or throttle down fast and hopefully go back to where you know deep water is.

The first time I ran aground was during a race. I was on the crew list with the Seattle Women's Sailing Association (SWSA), and received a call from a guy asking me to do a *Jack & Jill* race in Seattle. Only two people are allowed on the boat, one guy and one girl. I tried to get out of it because I really had no experience racing. I was totally intimidated by the prospect of having just two of us on the boat. He had a trimaran and assured me that he could single-hand the boat so I didn't need to worry. So I agreed to do it.

You are sure to be on rocks if you go aground in Puget Sound; it is not like in Florida, which has mostly sandy bottom. So there we were racing: he was at the helm and we were getting closer and closer to shore. I saw twenty-five feet on the depth sounder, which terrified me. He reassured me we were okay. He told me he was going to hand the helm off to me so he could take care of the sails when we tacked. I was told to wait until he told me to turn the tiller. All I had to do was follow his instructions.

Unfortunately, he told me too late and all of a sudden we were aground. I just started saying over and over in my mind, "Oh my gosh! Oh my gosh!" Then in an instant, I remembered that someone once told me that you are not really a sailor until you go aground, and I realized I had just been initiated. So now I was excited instead of fearful.

He got us out of there by pulling the centerboard up, but I forgot to turn the helm (I was clueless at the time) so we were being blown right back on to the rocks. He ran to the stern and pulled the rudder off too. We were now being blown away from the shore. In an instant the rudder and centerboard were back in place. We ended up taking third place even after all that!

Now, if you are hard aground, one way to get off a shoal is to use your anchor as a kedge. "Kedging off" means taking an anchor out to deep water and then using it to pull yourselves off the shoal. If you have a dinghy, you can carry the anchor out to deep water. It's not so easy without one. I have heard of people putting their Danforth, which is a lighter anchor, on a cushion and floating it out, while swimming. But I'm not sold on that idea. In any case, once you have the anchor set, you should be able to manually to pull yourself toward it. A windlass on the bow is usually not a very strong motor and you can quickly burn it out, so that is why I suggest doing it manually.

The other way to get unstuck is by asking a fellow boater or calling for assistance. When asking for a tow from someone you should always ask what they will charge you first. If you do not establish the payment, they can basically own your boat. This is called salvage rights. While I don't think it happens very often these days, it is something of which you should be aware. Most people, however, are just happy to help. Also, always give them your line rather than taking their line.

When I was single-handing, I ran aground once in the Bahamas. I was trying to get my boat into one of the hurricane holes in Georgetown. There is a reef that is only marked by a stick in the water. The breeze was picking up and gale force winds were expected. I over-shot the reef and ended up right on top of it. Within a few minutes there were at least four or five guys in their dinghies at my boat ready to help get me out of there. In less than twenty minutes I was safely anchored in the hurricane hole.

WHAT TO DO IF A LEAK DEVELOPS

The first thing to do if you spring a leak is get the bilge pump working, and then find the source of the leak and the extent of damage. Check all your through-hull fittings first as well as the stuffing box. You should have onboard tapered soft wood plugs. A lot of cruisers drill a small hole through one and run a string through it and tie it right to the through-hull fitting so the plug is right there in the event of an emergency.

All boats have scuppers that allow any water that gets into the cockpit to flow off the boat. Well my boat had a one-inch hose that ran from the scuppers to the cockpit drains. The hose had separated from the scupper and was lying down in the transom of the boat. When the boat heeled over, the drain was under water and this allowed the water to flow freely into the boat.

I thank God that I went down below when I did, because the bilge was already full. At least it hadn't flowed over the floorboards yet. It could quickly have become a more serious situation had we not found and resolved the problem rapidly. As it was, we ended up heading back to the Port Everglades inlet and motored down to Miami before it was dark. We went to the West Marine near Dinner Key marina the next day and two days later we made an uneventful passage across the Gulf Stream.

WHAT TO DO IF YOU DRAG ANCHOR

There are several factors that affect an anchor's ability to keep the boat in place. Too many people have no idea how much scope to put out when anchoring. They don't have their chain or rode measured and marked off, and then wonder why they have problems. They also don't have the correct amount of chain, which increases an anchor's holding power and makes it more reliable. Then there is the type of anchor to consider, and the bottom-type in which you are anchoring, subjects which I am not going to address; ask other cruisers what type they use in what bottom conditions (sand, rock, grass, mud, etc.), and read up on the different kinds of anchors to learn more and be better prepared.

The Coast Guard recommends that you have at least fifteen feet of chain. I don't agree with this number, but one of my neighbors on the dock, an old salt with a forty-foot Morgan Out Islander follows the Coast Guard guidelines. After researching and talking to a lot of people, my

recommendation is to have at least a boat-length of chain. Twice the length is even better, but all chain is best. Consider this: my neighbor has fifteen feet and I have fifty. He insisted that he was right because he follows regulations, but admitted to often dragging anchor. Even after living "on the hook" for almost six months, my anchor has never dragged. So the question is: how well do you want to sleep at night?

If your anchor is dragging, you should start by increasing the scope. Chances are if you don't have the 7-1 ratio out for overnight anchoring, your anchor may not do the job. A lot of times increasing the scope and using your engine to back down on the anchor will resolve the problem. You can also rig another anchor (if possible), and re-anchor when all else fails. Don't forget to take into consideration where you are in the tidal range and set the scope for high tide. A lot of seasoned sailors will also add the height of the freeboard to their ratio. (Freeboard is the height of the hull between the water line and the deck.)

There are tags with numbers that you can weave into the rode so you know how much scope you have out. I used waterproof markers and used three colors: one mark of black for 10 feet, a green for 20 feet and a red for 30 feet. I then started doubling the marks, 2 blacks for 40 feet, 2 marks of green for 50 feet, and so forth. You can do it even more easily by painting one mark at 25 feet, 2 marks at 50 feet, etc.

One anchoring hazard that nobody tells you about when you first start cruising is that other boaters don't always follow accepted guidelines. I had just moved my boat to Lee Stocking Island, which is across from Georgetown in the Exumas. That was the only place where you could get Reverse Osmosis (RO) water. You have to take water jugs to the beach and fill them up at Chat and Chills. (The year I was there it cost fifty cents per gallon.)

When I returned from the beach with my water jugs, the woman on the boat in front of me, *Dulcinea*, hollered out, "We have a lot of chain out." Here was another incident where I didn't know what I didn't know. Her comment made no sense to me so I politely said, "Okay!" and went about getting the boat filled with water.

I did notice that our boats seemed a little closer so I let out a little more scope and kept going. I was only spending one night there and then a girlfriend and I were going to visit some nearby islands. In the middle of the night, the wind kicked up. Thank God I was sleeping in the V-berth, because suddenly I heard a clunk. I jumped up and looked out of the hatch. That woman's boat was bearing down on me and her dinghy had bumped into my boat.

She came out on deck and said, "I told you I had a lot of chain out." We were only anchored in about 15 feet of water and she said she had about 200 feet of chain out. I asked her if she could take some of it up and her answer was an emphatic, "No!" I thought, "That was pretty rude of her," so I went and let out all of the rode that I had. I sat up watching for a long time, but never really slept well the rest of the night.

In the morning my girlfriend, Shelly, and her husband, Doug, came over in the dinghy to help me weigh anchor. As we started moving my boat forward we realized that we were headed for a collision with *Dulcinea*. Doug used the dinghy to push *Dulcinea* aside so I could motor my boat forward and pick up the anchor without hitting them. Of course by now the couple on *Dulcinea* was on deck and everyone was telling me what to do.

Things seemed to be going okay until I got to my anchor. Their chain had crossed over my anchor and it was caught. There was discussion of having someone dive to fix it. We decided to try one more time motoring forward and voila! It finally broke free. That experience taught me a lesson or two!

Georgetown is a convergence zone, so the weather from the Caribbean bumps into the weather coming down from Florida. Sometimes you swing in circles on your anchor. You may have started the night facing south but end up facing north by morning. You never know how much swinging around you may do in the night. That can also cause the chain to bunch up.

One morning, I was getting into my dinghy and was planning to be gone for the day when I noticed that I was right on top of someone's anchor. I was anchored in less than ten feet of water and because it was so clear it was easy to see the bottom. I could see the chain attached

to the anchor and I thought, "I'd better find out whose anchor this is because if they decide to pull it up, they will hit me." I didn't want to have to worry all day, so I used the dinghy to follow the anchor rode…all the way around right back to the bow of my own boat. That is what happens when you sit at anchor for any length of time and the winds change, causing your boat to swing around a lot. This taught me to always back down on my anchor if I am staying for any length of time in one place. No more anchor problems after that! In fact, it was eight years before I ever drug anchor again and that was in a big storm.

WHAT TO DO IF A HALYARD BREAKS

They say that the first thing to do if the halyard breaks is to secure the sail by pulling it down. It makes sense, since you could end up loosing the sail or ripping it, which can become costly. I have spare halyards for both jib and main already rigged. My spare main halyard acts as a topping lift and my spare jib halyard is also the spinnaker halyard. It works in an emergency and when I'm not using it, it's great for hooking up the wind scoop or hammock. (You gotta' have a little fun!)

When I was sailing to Tahiti, I read Herb Payson's book *Blown Home Again*. I started noticing a quirky correlation as I read. In one chapter, Herb described an alternator problem, and the next thing I noticed was that the guys on *Maya* were replacing the alternator. In the next chapter, Herb was replacing the impeller, and lo and behold! I noticed we were doing the same thing on *Maya*.

When I pointed out this parallel, one of the guys said, "I don't care what happens in that book, I'm not going up the mast!" This was a seventy-foot aluminum yacht and the mast was at least ninety feet tall. You wouldn't have gotten me up there in the middle of the ocean on a bet.

Our day started out with lighter winds and the owner decided to shake out the reef we took the night before. He used the electric winch to hoist the mainsail. He started cranking the electric winch, and nothing was happening so he pressed that button harder and you could hear the winch working hard but nothing was happening. Suddenly, we heard this big bang! He had accidentally left the halyard tied to a cleat, so the pressure of the electric winch finally snapped the halyard. Thank God it didn't break at the top of the mast. We were able to sew the two ends together and feed the new halyard up through the mast while pulling the old halyard out of the mast. Well, he didn't have to go up the mast, but we did end up with a similar problem to Herb's. Everyone wanted me to stop reading the book after that!

Being prepared and having spares is important. I have spares for both sails and halyards. You may never need them, but if you need spares and don't have them, no amount of regret will fix the problem.

WHAT TO DO IF THE PROPELLER FOULS

Without thinking too hard, I could come up with several stories I could tell you about a fouled propeller. We have run over crab pot lines during class trips multiple times. We've also had to sail into the dock because of seaweed fouled around the propeller.

There are some easy and smart ways to avoid this situation, but, of course, it requires an understanding of the wind. If I'm sailing between a string of crab pots, I will try to sail as close to the one of which I am leeward and as far away from the windward one as possible. The wind is always pushing the boat a lit bit sideways; that is why we say the boat is "crabbing." If something is to leeward of the boat, the wind is going to push us right into it. If I keep the obstacle to windward, and can see it, I will only get blown further from it.

Beginners often try to steer a boat like a car, but it doesn't work because a boat can pivot and round up. Also, we're not driving on a solid surface! This is a fluid environment and you need to recognize and respond differently to the wind conditions and currents in the water.

We have had several fouling incidents in the middle of sailing class, and here is what I teach the students to do. The first thing to do is to make sure you stop the engine immediately. If you do not, you may be paying a hefty price in engine repair work. There are several options after the engine is off. The easiest is, if the water isn't too cold, going overboard and disentangling the line from the propeller. This is the quick fix. Otherwise your choices are: use your tow insurance and call for help; use your dinghy to tow yourself back; or sail to the anchorage. One way or another you will need to cut that line away. There are always divers in marinas who do bottom-cleaning and who may be willing to help you. My diver, Joey, is always there to take care of things like that for me.

In places like Maine, because of the abundance of lobster pots, most boaters put a cage around their propeller. It's pretty cool and it's better than the blades cutting the lines so the fishermen don't loose their pots.

My first experience with getting a line fouled was while pulling up my anchor in the Bahamas. I thought I had my dinghy line tied up tight to the boat, but obviously it was not. Just as we were getting the anchor up, the engine suddenly started making a horrible noise. I shut the engine down immediately. In this case, we had to drop the anchor again and hope that it set. Since the water in the Bahamas is warm and clear, it was easy enough for us to jump in and untangle the line. In no time we were back on track and sailing out of the anchorage.

If you are at anchor and are simply going for a day sail, you can leave your dinghy tied to the anchor. Then you don't have to take either of them with you or worry about the line getting fouled. It's like returning to a mooring; it's much easier and it saves your spot.

WHAT TO DO IF A LINE FOULS AROUND THE RUDDER

This is not as severe a problem as a line around your propeller, but it is a big nuisance. Fixing it is as simple as just turning the wheel, or tiller, back and forth to jiggle the line free. The problem is, unless you can see the line drift away, you don't always know if you have been successful. You might have to go overboard to check it.

A local couple had come aboard *Tididi* to take their advanced classes. The intermediate and advanced classes cover the *what ifs* and problem-solving. They had found a Choe Lee, built back in the 1970's, and they were going to fix it up, live aboard and go cruising. We were returning from an overnight trip. We had a great time cooking dinner, laughing and getting to know each other. As we were coming up the Pass-a-Grille channel, the husband was at the helm and acknowledged a crab pot. I was thankful that he noticed it and told him that. Suddenly I heard an awful clunking and I said, "Quick, throttle down." He did and I said, "I think we caught the crab pot." Being a guy, he immediately denied running over it. This sort of defensiveness isn't helpful—it's better to just acknowledge it and deal with it.

I looked over where he had just said the pot was, and I didn't see anything. Obviously, we caught something! Students often forget about how the wind and current cause the boat to crab, and that is usually how they get into situations like this one. It is so important to keep checking and rechecking all the obstacles in the water. If you let your guard down, you won't know what hit you!

He said, "I think maybe if we put it into reverse we can get it off." He tried it and we could hear that awful *clunk, clunk, clunk.* We had no other option but to turn off the engine. I could not see the line or the float, so I had to assume that it was or soon would be fouled on my propeller. We were only a short distance from the bridge, and the only way to get there was to sail. We started short-tacking, making a series of quick zigzags, toward our destination. We did this without making much headway, and finally I realized that at the rate we were going, we would never get under the bridge.

Do you know the rule for sailors? Wherever it is that you want to go, that is where the wind is coming from. So, of course, the wind was coming from the bridge's direction. I decided that we would take a chance that the line was only around the rudder and use the engine just long enough to get us under the bridge. It worked—no clunking. The moment we got to through the bridge we shut the engine back down until we got to the channel to the marina. We did the same thing back into the slip.

Once we were safe at the dock I called the diver and asked him to come over to find the problem. Well, as you may have guessed, there was nothing there. With all that tacking we did, turning the rudder back and forth, we had broken the line free without realizing it. The

lesson here is to always be conservative until you know for sure that the problem is resolved.

Incidentally, the couple found this whole experience very upsetting. When things go wrong it can become overwhelming. The way people respond to problems tells a lot about them. This was something they could put in their story bank, but at the time, they were too upset to see the valuable lesson. The whole point of the class was to learn, first hand, what to do when things go wrong and how to appropriately handle problems. If you ever find yourselves in their position, remember that it is delusional to think that you will never face problems, particularly if you buy a thirty-year-old boat! Students who experience a boat problem in their class are the lucky ones. They get to experience the realities of sailing with someone who knows what to do and how to handle crises. It's better than learning the hard way, when you're out there on your own.

WHAT TO DO IF THE RIGGING FAILS

I am very thankful that I personally, have not been involved in a dismasting, but I have several professional captains and friends who have had it happen to them. To me, this is one of the scariest of all the potential problems that can happen.

If you are on a boat and rigging starts to fail, then I am sure you are in some pretty severe weather and rough seas. It may mean that you didn't do your weather planning correctly. Sometimes, despite the best planning, storms catch us off-guard.

My friend, Captain Dave, was the delivery captain for a new boat owner. Dave was at the helm dealing with a sever weather situation on the Chesapeake while the owner was down below losing his lunch. He and the other crew were all sea sick. I won't go into all of the details, however, Dave told me the weather got so bad that even the Coast Guard didn't want to come out and assist them. They all survived, but what a terrifying ordeal!

Captain Dave had told the owner he had some rigging problems that needed to be done before the trip. Having ignored his Captain's advice, he caused the demise of his own boat. The trip was memorialized on a plaque presented to Captain Dave by the owner, who had part of the rigging and lines incorporated into it. That certainly fits the male psyche! What you survive you can boast about. His plaque is a badge of honor. My hat is off to delivery captains, who are often at the mercy of owners' schedules and judgment calls.

Another friend of mine experienced a dismasting in a severe storm over a hundred miles off of Cape Hatteras. This time the Coast Guard did come out and evacuate them. The boat did survive; it floated to shore, stripped of its rigging. After fighting with the insurance to pay for the damaged boat, he sold the remains for a few thousand dollars.

So if you find a broken stay, or if a shroud breaks, make sure you quickly remove pressure from the damaged wire. Tack the boat if necessarily and luff the sails. You can use those spare halyards as temporary rigging—anything to keep your mast standing. I don't think I would try to sail using a halyard as rigging, but if it keeps you from losing the mast then it's done its job.

If you do get dismasted, have a wire cutter handy on the boat so that you can cut all the stays and free the mast and get it away from the boat so that it won't punch holes in your hull and potentially sink you. If you can save the mast, that is great, but don't lose your life over a hunk of metal.

WHAT TO DO IF THE STEERING FAILS

If you suddenly lose steerage, find an alternate method for steering the boat. Do you have an emergency tiller, or as some people call it, a rudder extension? I have talked to a lot of people who know they have one, but have no clue how to use it or what it takes to attach it. It doesn't help to have emergency equipment that you can't find or can't use in an emergency!

This is another one of those skills that you need to practice. How long would it take to regain control of your boat in the event of losing

steerage? I encourage you to find out before it happens. It should not be very difficult to rig up. Make sure it is always in the same place so you can find it in a hurry.

It wasn't until I started teaching that I finally took my rudder post extension out and figured out how to use it. My emergency tiller is on the right side of the port lazarette. To remove the access cap for the rudder post, I need a Phillip's head screwdriver. So I always keep one in the drawer below the navigation table. I can pull those two items out, have the cap off, and the emergency tiller attached in only a minute or two. This is why there is *a place for everything and everything in its place.*

Do you know how to use your sails to steer? If you have never sailed to the dock or on and off the anchor, it's a good idea to practice. This is one of the reasons, that learning to sail on a small boat is valuable. Once you can sail a small boat to the dock it's just as easy to sail a larger boat, although you need to take into consideration the additional momentum for the larger boat. You can adjust your sails to balance the boat and head into or away from the wind. You need both the mainsail and the jib to make it work.

I have taught classes for several schools in the St. Petersburg area. I told the owner of a school in Clearwater that the steering cable was loose on one boat and that he needed to get it fixed before the upcoming class. Whether it was repaired or not, we ended up losing the steering completely that following weekend.

The best part of that situation was that the students had just learned how to set the anchor and we had already talked about emergency situations. Suddenly we were doing a fire drill. I sent the wife to the bow to drop the anchor and the husband to get the emergency tiller. Within only a few minutes the boat was back under control. I was so proud of the way they handled the whole situation. It is so important to remember not to start panicking when things go wrong, but to trouble-shoot calmly.

WHAT TO DO IF YOU ARE GROUNDED AT ANCHOR

Once you are aground at anchor, the game is over. You have already blown it. Now the goal is to make sure the boat doesn't get damaged while waiting for the tide to come back up.

I got lucky the night we were going aground. Some folks on a boat named *Nomad,* decided to go into a shallow anchorage and have a bonfire on the beach. Several other boats joined in. The charts showed this place to be about two feet deep at low tide. I would never have thought of going in there in the first place, but when the tide was up we had plenty of water.

All was well until we returned to our boats to discover that we were all going aground. The tide was still falling and we had just enough water under our keels to bounce our way out of there. It was a close call.

A friend of mine wasn't so lucky when he was in the South Pacific. He ended up on a reef at one of the atolls. The problem with a full keel boat is that it doesn't right itself very easily once it's on its side. As the tide rolled in, the waves pushed the boat against the reef. All that crashing eventually caused a hole in the boat. It was a total loss in the end. This is a serious and scary situation in which to find yourself.

Keep checking those charts and tide tables, especially in unfamiliar places. And even more importantly, check and double check, in places with excessive tides. The further north you go, the greater the tides. Places like Seattle and Maine have ten to twelve foot tides and some places in Europe have as much as thirty to forty foot tides. Don't assume anything and don't guess.

WHAT TO DO IF SOMEONE GOES OVERBOARD

In almost every seriously dangerous situation I have heard or read about, you only have ten to fifteen minutes to save your life or that of someone else. So the time is now to prepare yourselves for the worst-case scenario. Don't be caught off guard. Your life and that of your mate is precious.

170

Do you have an abandon-ship drill? Do you practice at least once a year? Do you know where your emergency equipment is located—and even more important, how to use it? Do you know how to light a flare? Do you practice M.O.B. drills under both power and sail? If you don't, you should make all of these things a regular part of your seasonal sailing routine.

Your M.O.B. practice drills will most likely take place in the best of conditions and they should become as easy to you as riding a bicycle. I can almost guarantee that when a disaster really happens, the wind will be over twenty-five knots and the seas will be more than five feet high. And even worse, *what if* it happens at night? If you don't have these routines down so well that you can almost do them in your sleep, you are not truly prepared. You do not want the guilt that you will feel if someone loses his life because you did not take the time to prepare properly.

I cannot emphasize this enough: you will have less than fifteen minutes to deal with most true emergencies. This is why your lifesaving and emergency plans should be practiced on a regular basis. You truly are not a skilled sailor until you are proficient in M.O.B. drills. And captains, if you are not teaching all of your crew how to do the drills from the helm, it will be you who does not return.

When I was in New Zealand, in 2006, my friend, Rodger, and I were listening to the VHF radio when we heard a mayday call. We heard that the boater was hit by a whale. Unfortunately we were too far away to assist, but having seen a whale the day before we were even more on the lookout after that.

When we returned to shore, there was a big story in the newspaper about this guy on a fifty-foot boat that was hit by a whale. He said in the article that he had just enough time to get his grandkids into life jackets, grab his wife's purse and get everyone into the dinghy. He lost the entire vessel in about ten minutes. If that doesn't sober you up, nothing will!

Don't let these stories cause you to be so afraid that you don't go out and enjoy all that is wonderful about sailing and cruising. Instead, let them be lessons to you not to take anything for granted. Don't let your guard down and be proficient at emergency drills.

In a true man overboard situation, you will need to turn the boat around and be able to stop it, while keeping your eyes on the victim and preparing to retrieve him. You should have a Lifesling attached to the rails to make hauling a victim aboard easier. Because it has a polypropylene line attached, which floats, all you have to do is get it to the victim. You don't have to try and sail up to the victim in eight foot seas and stop. Once the victim has the line, he is now attached to the boat. All you have to do is heave to, and pull the victim to you. If you have a ladder on your transom, they can climb back on board. If the victim is injured, you may have to rig a hoist. Knowing how to do these things ahead of time eliminates a lot of the panic. People stop thinking clearly when they panic. If a child goes into the water, it is likely one parent will go in after the child, but it is advisable that they tell someone before doing so! As a man overboard can happen under sail or power, you should practice both ways until you are comfortable.

One last thing on M.O.B. drills, once you know how to sail, how to handle your boat and put it on a specific point of sail, doing M.O.B. drills are a blast. It's fun and challenging. And there shouldn't have to be anything scary about doing drills—the worst thing that can happen is that you will loose a cushion. Please don't practice with real people in the water; someone could get hurt and turn your practice emergency into a real one. But use an occasion like a hat blowing overboard as an opportunity to practice.

WHAT TO DO IF THERE'S A FIRE

Are you aware of all the types of fuel that can cause fires aboard? Why should you care? How about in case of a fire? Again, a boat will burn to the waterline in ten to fifteen minutes.

Are you aware of the potential causes for fire aboard? Alcohol, propane or compressed natural gases in cooking stoves top the list. CNG is lighter than air so it accumulates at the top of a cabin while propane and gas fumes are heavier and will sink down into the bilges. Always sniff the bilge before starting a gasoline engine. Inboard diesel engines are less likely to cause a fire than your gasoline outboard motor. You might have kerosene in heating and lighting fixtures. Did you know that there is methane in your holding tank? And hydrogen gas in your batteries? All of these things are flammable and can cause your vessel to burn and sink in less than fifteen minutes! Are you prepared?

To prevent fires and/or explosions on a boat, it's important to ventilate all areas of potential fire or explosion. What are the types of fires? Do you know how to use a fire extinguisher? How many extinguishers do you have and where are they located? You should be able to answer these questions.

Learn your *A-B-C's* to remember the three types. Type A is for ASH; you are extinguishing paper or wood fires. Type B is for BOIL; this is for gasoline, oil, and grease fires. Type C is for CURRENT; the most dangerous are electrical fires. (The quicker you remove the source of electricity, the less chance of getting electrocuted.)

AN OUNCE OF PREVENTION IS WORTH A POUND OF CURE

I'm not trying to be the bearer of bad news here, but we all hear the stories, and read the books written by those who were fortunate enough to survive. What about those people who were lost and never heard from again?

You should always do your preventative maintenance. You are checking through-hulls in the boat to prevent possible leaks so the boat won't sink. You are checking the standing rigging so that the mast will stay standing up. You are always working on the engine to make sure you can get into a safe harbor and out of a storm.

Ladies, show appreciation for your husband when you see him doing what you think is tinkering on the boat. He is making sure your boat is shipshape and safe. Let him tinker to his heart's content if it means you are going to be able to sail safely. And kudos to you guys who love to do it.

If you are not building your skills and learning how to handle emergencies, you are not truly ready to go cruising. Those fears and apprehensions are valid. The new STCW training, required by all professional crew traveling in international waters, is advanced emergency training and preparation. When I traveled to Europe as a guest aboard the *Michaela Rose*, I was still required to participate in the emergency practice drills. I was required to know where the fire extinguishers and the life jackets were. That Captain was responsible for my life and responsible for making sure I was prepared to survive any emergency. While you may not have twelve crew members aboard your boat, you should always have everyone onboard familiar with where emergency equipment is located and how to use it—including a guest who may only be there for a day- sail.

The yacht on which I sailed to Tahiti had an extensive emergency medical kit. We spent over an hour reviewing what was in the medical kit. Every item was explained to us—what it was for, how to use it, and where to find instructions. We were taught what to do if we had to stitch someone up or even do minor surgery, like a tracheotomy, although they said we should not do it unless we had a doctor walking us through the process. (Duh!) Yet we never once practiced an M.O.B. drill. Yikes! *What if* something bad had happened? I don't know how well any one of those guys would have done in an emergency like that out on the Pacific. It is scary to think about.

There are companies that will put together custom medical kits for cruisers. They automatically ship you fresh medicines when yours expire. They have company representatives who are nurses and can help advice you on putting together the right medical kit.

My safety talk, which includes all of the Coast Guard required equipment, can be quickly recalled with the acronym, *Fun People Sail Nicely.* Take the first letter in each word and remember these items:

F is for fire extinguishers and flares. Know where they are and how to use them. Discuss and demonstrate these things when possible.

P is for PFD's, or personal floatation devices. Know the types for each person on board, where they are located, and how to put them on. You should always have them accessible from the cockpit. Believe it or not, some people don't even know how to use the throw-able Type IV properly. If you don't have a Lifesling, get one! Don't pass go until you have one on board. This is the best device for a real M.O.B. situation.

S is for Ship's papers and sound-producing device. If the Coast Guard boards you, the first thing they will ask for is your proof of ownership. It is just like getting pulled over in a car. So, keep your registration or documentation in the same place and in a waterproof container. You will also need it to get through customs, if you travel outside the country.

Most people will carry only a canister-type air horn, but half the time it is stowed in a locker somewhere down below. Your horn should be accessible from the helm. What good does it do you if you need it and you have to run down below to dig it out? By the time you find it, you could be having the collision you were trying to prevent. And believe me; they are not going to hear you hollering, if they are in a boat with the engines roaring. The other problem with the canister-type horn is that it will only last for a short period of time. I was caught in fog, two mornings in a row, while coming back from Key West. The law requires a boat to make the proper sound signal every two minutes. It doesn't take long before you are out of air! I have a manual horn that will keep blowing until my last breath. They also now make a rechargeable pump-type air horn.

N is for Navigation lights and Navigation Rules of the Road. I've had some people tell me that as a pleasure boater you are not required to have a copy of the rules on board and that it only applies to the professional boaters. I disagree. I think it is even more important for the casual sailor to have them, especially if you are a part-time boater. Professional captains are on the water all the time and applying the rules all the time. Pleasure boaters may only go out occasionally, and because they are not using the rules all the time, chances are they will have forgotten them. When you are only on the water for a few months out of the year, it is easy to forget. What you don't use, you lose.

A safety talk before you go sailing only takes a few minutes, but can save lives. All professional mariners do this, so why not follow suit?

In my seminars and in the 2x2 Micro Method book; I have some easy mnemonics and acronyms to help everyone remember the rules of the road and aids to navigation. Mnemonics make memorization easy and fun.

HAVE A PLACE FOR EVERYTHING AND EVERYTHING IN ITS PLACE

There is nothing more frustrating than looking for something you really need on your boat and not finding it. You know exactly where it's supposed to be, but now you can't find it.

I know you may think this is silly, but it is one of my pet peeves. An example is where I keep the lighter for the BBQ. It's not in the typical place that most people would keep it. I have mine in the bin with all of my cooking utensils, like the spatula and ladle. It doesn't matter how many times I tell people to put things back where they belong, the lighter sometimes ends up elsewhere. Of course, when I need it, I won't be able to find it. I will search high and low for it and when I don't find it, I end up buying another one. Eventually someone will discover the lighter—and sometimes in the oddest places. I'm at the point where I just laugh about it. Human nature is like that. I just don't sweat the small stuff anymore.

Some people get neurotic about this guideline. If someone is obsessing, it becomes unpleasant to sail with that person. If this is you, lighten up, okay? Yes, being shipshape is important, but becoming fanatical is annoying. You don't want people calling you Captain Bligh behind your back. So if this is you, ease up a bit. Life is too short to go overboard, so to speak. As with most things, there needs to be a balance. If someone removes that screwdriver and I need it because I lost my steering, I will be extremely upset. But the lighter incident is not that big of a deal. If you are sailing with other people, be respectful of their boat, their stuff, and their rules.

And skipper, if there are some things that are major to you, make sure that you emphasize that when talking to your crew. If you don't share your expectations ahead of time, then you don't have the right to be upset with them later. If there are things that are a must, write them down so people can refer to the list later. Otherwise, have a little fun!

KNOW WHERE YOU ARE AND KEEP YOUR EYES ON THE ROAD

Women are actually the best navigators. I'm not saying men are bad at it, but most women take to navigation like a duck to water. It comes natural for women to want to know where they are at all times. When you are in the car, who gets the map out? She does. So this job usually fits them like a glove; most women tell me they love doing it.

The problem with all jobs is that we may make mistakes. When you are plotting courses, finding and plugging waypoints into your GPS, make sure you check, recheck and then have your partner check it again. Don't take it as an insult if you check and recheck the coordinates with each other. Duplication makes for good navigation. You are not questioning the other person's ability to do the job; you are just doing your CYA work. There is nothing worse than thinking you are

in one place and ending up on the rocks because someone transposed a number in the waypoint.

When we were coming into Chub Cay, in the Bahamas, I did just that. I transposed a number and suddenly things just didn't look right. We started checking the charts, re-plotted our position and, sure enough, I had made a mistake. With that, we started updating our position on the paper chart every fifteen minutes until we knew for sure exactly where we were. There isn't an obvious channel into Chub Cay, and there are rocks, so we didn't have room for mistakes. The Bahamas are the worst when it comes to buoys and aids to navigation, so you'd better know where you are.

A word on those beautiful, wonderful, exciting, fancy chart plotters and computer charts: they can get you into a whole lot of trouble. They are great. I love them. But in the event of an emergency, when the power is out and those instruments don't work anymore, paper charts are worth their weight in gold. There was a letter in the Seven Seas

Cruising Association's monthly bulletin from a single dad traveling with his kids on their fifty-foot sailboat. He admitted in the article that his navigation skills were minimal, but he had the best of the best computer charts aboard and was confident they would be okay. Or should I say *over*confident?

Many cruising people will travel in packs from anchorage to anchorage. You are still on your own for the most part, but you always have others who are at least in hearing range if not visible, too. The good part about traveling in flotillas is that there are always other boats close by to help if you get out of (or into) trouble. I did the same thing while single-handing. Paul, another single-hander, buddy-boated with me until we got to Nassau. It was very reassuring for me to know he was close by and available if I needed help. But that should not lead to complacency; you must still endeavor to be self-sufficient.

Unfortunately, for the single dad using his fancy computer charts, they ended up on the rocks or coral near the Turks & Caicos. I think it had something to do with them navigating from down below, rather than having at least one pair of eyes on deck watching. Thank God that everyone survived, but I heard the boat was a total loss. That could be considered extremely negligent. I have heard many similar stories where people are relying on other people, and not using their own eyes. Things change, sand shifts and that is why charts are continuously updated. You are not always where you think you are, because of set and drift (i.e. wind and current). That is why I said above, check and recheck. Again, make no assumptions. It always gets you into a lot of trouble.

STANDING WATCHES

Your eyes are your most important asset when trying to keep the boat safe. When standing watches at night, make sure you give yourself time to prepare before you take over the watch. Check the charts, get an update from the person you are relieving. Do your personal businesses before you take over the helm: get your life jacket or harness ready, go to the bathroom, and get your drinks and snacks. It is your responsibility

to set your alarm and be on deck before your watch, so that you can get a briefing from the person whose shift is ending. Be awake, alert and prepared both physically and mentally before you take over. Everyone's life is depending on you to watch and stay awake.

Don't leave the helm unless necessary, and don't do other things like read books or play computer games. Playing music loudly or listening with headphones can also distract you and prevent you from hearing something you might need to hear. You are there to watch and listen for other vessels that could take your life. This means you need to know the light configurations for the various types of ships.

If you see a ship, you'll need to be able to answer questions like these. Is the ship going to cross your bow, if you see two white lights and a red light coming from your starboard side? Are you looking at the port or starboard side of that ship? Are you on a collision course? Do you know how to use your hand-held compass to take bearings a minute or two apart and find out?

If you are on watch at night, and you see something and you are not sure if it is a problem, wake someone up! Don't wait and don't worry if he gets upset with you. Your life is more important than someone losing a little bit of sleep. At the same time, try not to overreact, and ask your question in a calm and reasonable tone.

For those who are taking beginners on an overnight trip, try to match a new person with a more experienced person. One can be sleeping in the cockpit, while the other person watches so that the person on watch has immediate assistance if necessary. New people have to learn somehow. Don't be negligent and leave someone on deck who doesn't know what he is doing. And have that waterproof Rules of the Road card handy!

You never have to sail short-handed when you are making long passages. You can go on the Seven Seas Cruising Association's web site and put out a request for crew to help you make the trip. There are a lot of people who would love the opportunity to make a passage. And if you want to sign up as crew on someone else's passage, it is a great opportunity to try it before you do it on your own boat.

Two on a Boat How to Keep it Afloat

John Neal and Amanda Swan Neal take people on their boat, Mahina Tiare, for offshore training trips. You get to do your first ocean passage with people who have extensive experience. They teach you all the right things to do in emergencies, and prepare you so you can make your own successful passages. It really does help to do some training with experienced people the first time. It will remove much of fear and anxiety associated with ocean passages. (You can find them at www.mahina.com. They also offer a cruising seminar at the Seattle, Chicago and Oakland Boat Shows when they are not off cruising around the world.)

Standing your watch properly can save lives. One of the guys on Maya left the pilot house while on his watch. He decided he would make himself some coffee. We had weather warnings of some squalls with thirty five mph winds in them. I had objected to sailing wing and wing (a down-wind sail configuration) because of the weather report, but being the low man on the totem pole, or should I say "low woman," everyone ignored my warning.

We were hit by one of those squalls. Our mainsail had a preventer on it, and the jib was poled out with the spinnaker pole. When the boat broached, and the pole broke, it sounded like a bomb went off. That had to be the most frightening experience I had on the whole trip. That twenty-eight-foot carbon fiber spinnaker pole broke in two places. All hands were on deck in moments and it didn't take long to get the boat back under control. The spinnaker pole was dumped over board. And that is all I will tell you about listening to a woman's instincts. You can believer her or not, but it will be hard for her to resist saying, "I told you so."

It is true that standing night watches can be tiring, but they have an upside, too. Sailing at night is amazing. On a clear night, when away from lights on land and other obstructions, the stars are incredibly bright and beautiful. I was in awe the first time I saw the Southern Cross during the trip from Seattle to Nuka Hiva. What unforgettable things will you see? You'll have to get out there to find out.

Although much can go wrong on a boat, if you are well-equipped and prepared, you need not fear. Men and women tend to argue when a crisis arises because they handle emergencies differently. Sometimes a woman must trust a man's quick judgment in a dangerous situation, and sometimes the man must listen to his mate's intuitive warnings. As with so many other things, it is about balance. The worst thing they can do is use their energies to fight each other instead of fighting for their survival. Since a woman seems to need more time to process, she must make up for her lack of quick-thinking with preparedness. A woman loves to be prepared—just ask to see the contents of her purse! If you work as a team and practice for emergencies, expecting the unexpected, you will be ready when it occurs.

TWO ON A BOAT How to Keep it Afloat

TWELVE

DOCKING & ANCHORING DANCE

...the perfect little parking place is easy to find
all you really gotta do is read his mind
if what your honey wants is hard to tell
when the hand signals fail you can always yell
grind your teeth, shout till you're hoarse
there's always one more step, you can file for divorce
no better way to test a true romance
than to do, do, do, do, do
do the anchoring dance

ease to starboard, then hard to port
throttle down but you come up short
up on the foredeck, see them prance
when they do, do, do, do, do
do the anchoring dance...

The Anchoring Dance, (Used with permission from the CD *No Significant Features* by Eileen Quinn. Visit www.eileenquinn.com for more great cruising music.)

Eileen has a great way of putting into words what we all feel. Sound carries over water a little too well sometimes, and if you are spewing cruel and unkind words to each other in the process of docking or anchoring, you become the entertainment for the hour.

Eileen once used my little anchoring dance as the introduction to her *Anchoring Dance* song on the beach in Georgetown. I was terribly embarrassed about the incident at the time, but now it's minor in the grand scheme of things. So here is my anchoring dance story.

I had injured my back pulling my anchor up the wrong way, so for a while I would have to call friends in the anchorage to help me move my boat. I knew Eileen was going to be singing that night and wanted to be closer to the festivities, so I called another guy who was also single-handing to help me. The distance between Georgetown and Stocking Island is only about a mile and a quarter, but I was not comfortable taking my dinghy all that way. It was much easier for me to move the big boat so I would be closer after the evening events.

Brian met me on the Stocking Island side in his dinghy, pulled up alongside of my boat, and jumped aboard. We motored over near Chat & Chills so I could get in as close to shore as possible. He had put his handheld radio in his back pocket and just as he was supposed to put my anchor down, he decided he'd better move his radio so it didn't fall overboard. Well, of course, he bumped it and it went rolling off the deck and into the water, just as he had feared.

He immediately pulled his shorts off and was ready to jump off the boat to chase it. I saw this and yelled, "Don't you leave without putting my anchor down first!" He realized the radio was already a lost cause and finished helping me get my anchor down. Then he stripped naked and jumped overboard to retrieve the radio anyway.

I thought I would die of embarrassment. Everyone in the anchorage knew I was single-handing and here was this guy, getting naked on my boat in the busiest part of the anchorage, and in broad daylight. How could he do this to me? I quickly gave him a towel as he climbed up my stern ladder and scolded him for what he had done. I looked around hoping nobody had seen it all. Of all the people in the anchorage to see, it was Eileen. To my humiliation, the event was described, in detail, to the entire anchorage that night. We were the highlight of the evening's entertainment. The only saving grace was she didn't tell everyone my boat name.

The problem with anchoring and docking is that sound carries very well over water, so you are broadcasting everything you say for all to hear. Now everyone knows how you treat each other and the kind of people you are under pressure. No one is going to say anything, but think about how people are going to be looking at you.

Everyone who's done any cruising, or at least some anchoring, is familiar with the scene of the couple yelling at each other as they are putting the anchor down. By the time the anchor is set, you have two

people who are very unhappy with each other and everyone else in the anchorage knows about it too. You might be saying, 'been there done that!' Well, the good news is that you don't have to be that couple anymore. There are many little secrets to doing things together on a boat so you can sail together in peace and harmony and look just like a pro.

When it comes to yelling, I want you to remember something: it is the yeller who is considered the "bad guy", and not the person being yelled at. Don't forget that. They know your business and what kind of people you are by the way you do your anchoring dance. Your ability to anchor or dock a boat proves your capabilities as well as your experience. It is ultimately the helmsman who is responsible for stopping the boat, not the crew with the anchor or lines. The crew is there to assist and help secure the boat.

ANCHORING

During the entire time that I single-handed my boat, *not one time did I ever yell at myself.* So I'm thinking that if I can do this by myself, and not yell, what is all the yelling about?

As I've mentioned in a previous chapter, non-verbal communication is very effective when you are at the opposite end of the boat, particularly a big boat. Also, more and more couples are using headsets so they can discuss any issues that are happening while anchoring, and they appear so experienced because they do it so quietly. Because of my own experience with Brian, I would recommend the headsets over the handheld radios.

One of the problems when it comes to anchoring is the difference in perspective with distance. When I first started anchoring my boat I was always miles away from everyone else, and when boats got into my *personal space* I would get upset. The perception of distance is very different from the boat than it is from ashore. When I went ashore and saw the amount of distance I really had, I realized I made a big fuss about nothing.

There are a lot of ways to anchor. The Mediterranean moor, which is

anchoring and then backing the boat to the dock, is common in Europe, the South Pacific and the Caribbean, to name a few places. Taking a line to shore and doing a stern tie to a tree is done frequently in the Pacific Northwest because the anchorages are deep and the cliffs steep. Getting familiar with the area is important.

As long as you use the same anchoring strategy (i.e. Bahamian versus single anchor) as the other boats in the anchorage, everyone should swing together. Sometimes conflicts occur, such as if one boat puts out way too much scope. The more crowded the anchorage the less polite people are, so take care of yourself because nobody else will. If you don't like a situation, then you need to move. Don't expect them to move, even if you were there first.

Women aren't typically known for their judgment of distance. A guy finally informed me that the reason guys can gauge distances is from watching football. I gotta' tell you, I just don't see it. It's another one of those things that men see as clear as day, and it's a mystery to women. So don't ask a woman to drive the boat fifty yards then stop it. Most women will cringe and say, "Just tell me when you want me to stop." She is clueless. I'm clueless. But an easy solution is to use boat lengths. I understand and can visualize my own boat. I can estimate two or three lengths of my own boat. Just make sure you are using your own boat length, not someone else's boat length.

If your partner doesn't understand the whole anchoring process, it can be very confusing for her if you drop the anchor right between two other boats. She'll think, "What are you nuts, we'll hit each other!" If she understands that the end result will be your boat drifting back and moving far away from those other boats, you will avoid a lot of that yelling and arguing.

You should also agree on who is going to make that decision about where you will stop and drop the anchor. Is it the person at the bow, or the person at the helm? I get a mixed response when I ask this question at seminars. My preference is the person at the bow, because they have a better perspective of the anchorage and other boats. But it will more likely be the person with the most experience. In any case, make the agreement ahead of time instead of in the middle of the process.

Otherwise, when you don't agree the whole anchorage will know about it. Also, decide ahead of time who will be driving and who will be dropping! Both people should feel comfortable at the helm or at the bow, so practice both ways.

There are whole books written on the technicalities of anchoring, but there are three basic steps: 1) get head to wind and stop the boat's forward motion, and make sure the engine is in neutral once the boat stops; 2) get the anchor and enough scope on the bottom as quickly as you can, so the anchor will start grabbing; 3) once the boat blows back with the bow into the wind, back down with a little reverse throttle. That's it. All that yelling for something as simple as 1-2-3!

ON-THE-LEE VERSUS IN-THE-LEE

If you anchor on a lee shore, you may be in danger of drifting onto the rocks and wrecking your vessel. Again, this is where understanding the wind really helps. You want to anchor in-the-lee where the land, trees, hills, etc., will provide protection from wind and chop. The seas are calm and the boat is being blown away from the beach. If you do drag anchor, you will drift out into deeper water. If you are anchored on-the-lee you are being blown onto the beach and if you drag anchor you will go aground. Not a pretty picture.

In a convergence zone, like Georgetown, you can be anchored in-the-lee in the evening, but then the wind may shift and by the next morning you are on-the-lee. This is another good reason not to sit too long in one spot without getting things readjusted, like backing down on your anchor to reset it once in a while.

A friend of mine flew in from Florida to hang out with me while I was single-handing. We got up one morning and noticed that the weather was dreary. It was overcast and blustery. But we decided to go ashore any way.

We took my dinghy to the beach and noticed there wasn't another dinghy in sight. We wondered where everyone was. We decided to go see if *Chat and Chills* was open, and when we opened the door, the place was packed with people. We were shocked. Where were their dinghies? Well, it didn't take long for us to find out. A couple of kids came running into the pub and yelled, "Someone's dinghy is getting swamped."

About ten people went running out with my girlfriend and me, because we knew it was our dink. Sure enough, the waves were washing over the side of the inflatable and filling it up quickly. A bunch of the guys lifted the dinghy up and drained the water out. Then we put the motor down to see if it would start. Thank goodness it did. Then they showed me where all the others had put their boats—on the leeward side of the island. Not the best way to learn in-the-lee versus on-the-lee. Chalk it up to another incident where *I didn't know what I didn't know.* Ignorance is not bliss; it will get you into real trouble. So now I know, and so do you.

DOCKING

Docking can go very smoothly and quietly with a little discussion and pre-planning. Where is the wind? How is the current affecting you? Are the lines on the dock accessible? Are the lines and fenders aboard ready? Does the crew understand what they are expected to do? What line goes first and what line second? Have the crew done it before? What happens when there is nobody to catch the lines for you on the dock? Don't think someone will always be at the dock to help, and even if there is, they may be more trouble than help! (I don't believe you should ever relinquish your boat to strangers.)

When it comes to docking, the guy is usually at the helm and the woman is the crew doing what she is told to do, even if she doesn't really know or understand what she is doing. It amazes me that once a woman understands the process, she becomes both a great helmsman and feels better when assisting as crew.

I always tell my students, if you remember that most people can only retain three things in their short-term memory, then you can almost guarantee they will do something wrong, because there are at least a dozen things you need to keep in mind when you are docking. That is why if you give people driving directions and there are only three turns, they don't need to write it down, but the minute you give them a fourth turn they will forget everything unless it is on paper.

Docking practice is an opportunity to learn from your mistakes. I see so many boats at every marina that never leave the dock, and my theory is that they are afraid of leaving and coming back! Leaving a dock can be just as scary as coming back. If people spent just a little time practicing or taking docking lessons, they would probably actually go sailing more often. If you look at the cost of having a boat and divide it by the number of times that it actually leaves the dock, it would be much more cost effective for some people to charter rather than own a boat.

So how do you get better at docking and leaving the dock? How about just doing it? I always like to do a briefing before leaving and then a debriefing upon returning to the dock. What worked and what didn't? Ask lots of questions. How is the wind and current going to affect us? What could we have done differently? Did we discuss the possibilities ahead of time? Did something change with the wind or did we forget something? Are we being flexible enough and changing the plan when things aren't working out as expected? What is plan A and plan B? (You should always have an escape plan.) What dock lines could we have used to assist us? No blame, no arguments, just *what if and what's next*? If it didn't go well, try again until you get it down like clockwork.

Often when doing our docking practice, if the boat doesn't get close enough for the person on the bow to get their lines I will watch them just stand there waiting and doing nothing. I've seen both men and women respond this way. I always remind them that they are to watch each other's back and ask when you need help. Do something rather than nothing. It is too easy to be looking down at what you are doing and not notice the problem at the opposite end of the boat.

Typically the person at the bow is waiting for the boat to get close enough, and the person at the stern has already left the helm. The helmsman forgot to take the boat out of reverse, and now the boat is getting further from the dock instead of closer. Because the crew at the bow can't reach their lines they will stand there bewildered. That's the deer in the headlights syndrome. Don't be afraid to yell *TO* the helmsman, "Hey what's up? I need help here!"

The crew at the bow should not be afraid to ask for what they need, even if it is just asking what to do next. The person at the helm shouldn't forget their crew. Look up once in a while to make sure that all is well at the other end of the boat. Always be ready to stop what you are doing and implement Plan B. Leave the helm and go assist the other person on the other end of the boat if necessary.

As you have learned, I don't mind sharing my own mistakes because maybe, just maybe, you can learn something from them and now you can avoid the consequences. Mind you, it will be easy enough to accumulate your own mistakes, just hopefully not the same ones. We learn by evaluating our mistakes in boating, as in life, and then changing course. Why is it that as adults we forget this? We often expect perfection, but it just doesn't exist.

When I hear comments like, "*I thought* you said . . ." it tells me that someone didn't go through the whole discussion process, and he isn't taking responsibility for what he did wrong in the process. The more you review the situation as part of the learning process, the more ideas you can come up with to add to the arsenal. This is how you find a better way to handle the same situation in the future. By doing this, it will not only give you new ideas to use in the future, but nobody has to feel bad, even if it didn't go as smoothly as you wanted it to.

So ask yourselves, "What has worked before in this situation? Did we discuss the possibilities and how to handle them ahead of time? Does everyone know their job?" I can't emphasize enough to always be thinking, *what if and what's next*?

Once again, if you want to be a good helmsman, learn how to be good crew first. When you've made mistakes first, you will be better at giving commands and instructions, and you will remember what it is like to be on the receiving end. You will know what your crew has to deal with, and see what your partner is up against as crew. It will totally change your perspective as the helmsman and help you to communicate more clearly to the crew.

There are also inherent tendencies in a boat, like the direction the propeller is going to spin when you put the gear in reverse. Do you know

whether you have a prop that pulls to port or to starboard? Don't untie the dock lines until you know what your boat is going to do in reverse.

I was teaching a class aboard another captain's boat and the captain said to the students, "You never know what the boat is going to do in reverse." I interrupted and said, "I beg to differ." I always know what my boat is going to do because first, I know its inherent tendencies; second, I look at how I am being affected by the wind and current; and finally, I make a plan before I ever start untying dock lines."

Because the water is washing away from the rudder when the propeller is in reverse, you need more throttle when you are first backing out to create water flow that will give you some steerage with the rudder.

The last lines to release are always the windward side and the first lines to pick up when returning are the windward side. When you favor the windward side, you give yourself some room for error.

Your assertiveness with the throttle needs to match the wind's aggressiveness. If the wind is light, don't use as much throttle. In stronger winds, if you don't use more throttle the wind will take over and wreak havoc on the process very quickly.

If the wind is coming from abeam, you need to be aware of how that wind will affect your bow. Since the bow is lighter, the wind can catch it and blow it the wrong way.

When you stop and evaluate all the possible factors that will affect your boat's movement, you can make a plan. I have both the helmsman and the crew hold their windward lines and keep holding the dock line until the boat is actually moving. This gives you a way to recover the boat if things are not working the way you expected. And if a surprise boat pops out of nowhere, you can stop and regroup. You can't do that if you have already released your dock lines.

You can also use lines to warp off the pilings. Dock lines are used for both leaving the dock and returning. So don't just throw the lines without a plan if the wind suddenly catches you off guard. And don't forget to check for traffic one more time before you pull out of your slip. There is nothing worse than being caught off-guard by a sudden crisis when you are half way out of your slip.

When I teach docking class, first we go out into the bay and do our M.O.B. cushion recovery maneuvers. Learning how to stop and maneuver your boat is much easier when there are none of those hard things like docks, pilings, or other people's boats to hit. Stopping a boat under power works the same for an M.O.B. maneuver as it does for picking up moorings, anchoring, and, most importantly, for docking. So when you want to learn how to dock, do it with a cushion in the middle of the bay first, where you cannot hurt anyone or anything.

It is the responsibility of the helmsman to stop a boat. That means it is NOT the crew's responsibility to stop a boat! A good helmsman will use the throttle, neutral and reverse, to stop the boat. Too many people get hurt trying to pull on dock lines, or use their bodies and limbs to fend off the dock. That is completely unnecessary! You should not depend on the crew to use the dock lines to stop the boat. Too often the person at the helm has not taken into consideration how the boat is being affected by the wind and current, or worse, he just forgot what gear the engine is in. Nothing is worse than being blown into the slip. If you don't use enough reverse throttle to counteract wind or momentum, the boat will be creating a new imprint on the dock. If this happens, by the way, yelling about it after the fact will not repair the damage but add insult to injury.

Women have a secret weapon that actually makes them better at docking than some guys. What is that secret? It is the thing that she sees as a weakness that is actually her strength. Her secret weapon is...that she is slow! She is intimidated by the process of docking the boat, and worried about hitting something or damaging the boat, so she will come into the slip very slowly. That is the key! Did you miss it? It's going S-L-O-W-L-Y!

Don't become distracted because you think people are watching you. Worrying about messing up your docking maneuver will make you even more nervous, and then you will not make clear decisions. Oh, how I could go on with all the things that can go wrong when docking! Even with the best laid plans, it only takes one thing to make it go awry. And anyone watching on the dock has his own disaster story to tell, so they are usually commiserating rather than criticizing.

I like to teach the *touch and go method, as* opposed to the way I learned, the *crash and burn method.* I learned how to single-hand docking my boat by using an amidships line. When couples use an amidships line, it does two things for you. First, you are standing at the shrouds so you have something to hold onto as you step, not jump, off the boat. Second, when you tie off the amidships line as short and tight as you can, the boat is under control with that one line. The bow can't swing out and neither can the stern. Now it's not a crisis to come into the fuel dock or the transient dock. When you can dock a boat with only one dock line, the docking doesn't have to feel like such a stressful event every time.

☾

It's easy to get angry when things aren't going as planned. And uncontrolled anger can turn a mistake to be learned from into a relationship disaster. Both men and women must learn to laugh at the blunders instead of ruining the beginning or end of a trip together. I've given the run-down on basic anchoring and docking, but it behooves you both to spend time reading, talking, and practicing so that the whole process will be a lot less intimidating.

Two on a Boat How to Keep it Afloat

THIRTEEN

Steps Toward Resolving
the Battle of the Sexes

Respect is mandatory and it is a two-way street. Our motives for doing things are different. He is motivated by adventure, and she by safety and security.

One couple I had on my boat had named their alter egos. Let's say they called them Harold and Maude. When he was doing something that she didn't like, she would complain to her husband about "Harold." Because it wasn't a direct insult or put down to him, he was able to process that information from an objective vantage point. He could then make adjustments without offense to his personal ego. I thought this was a great way to deal with problems. They were funny to watch and fun to be with because they didn't really argue or hurt each other with insults. They were able to convey the problem to the other person without offense, and then adapt or correct the behavior. They had figured out a way to avoid the vicious battle of the sexes.

ᙚ

The more time I have spent researching gender differences, the more I have learned about basic human nature. The dynamics between men and women have been going on since Adam and Eve. Scientific studies have shown that our gender-related behavior traits are coded in our genes.

In the Bible, it is written that God designed men and women differently. The masculine and feminine traits are equally part of the "character of God." It is not just one or the other, but the two combined that create the whole, or the yin and the yang, if you want to look at it that way. I think that is why some couples feel that they are complete when they are together.

I debated whether I should include this chapter in the book because now I sound like a marriage counselor. I am not trying to tell you what to do, and I'm not a professional counselor, but just an observer of human nature. My classes with couples are usually part sailing technique and part relationship technique! The goal on a boat and in life should always be to work together as a harmonious team.

MEN'S NEEDS, WOMEN'S NEEDS

I have learned a lot about why my own relationship did not work out with Jack. It was that he cared more about what he wanted than about meeting my needs. There was an imbalance because I did not feel that I received the love and adoration that I needed. To be perfectly honest, I think he was more in love with himself than with me.

With Didier, it was a battle for status. I wanted for us to share the boat as equal partners. It didn't matter to me that I owned the boat, but it mattered to him. He felt that he was in a subservient or submissive role, which was a huge blow to his fragile male ego. I couldn't get him to see why I thought an equal partnership was an acceptable alternative to a hierarchy.

What went wrong in both cases? A failure to understand the basic needs of men and women. There is nothing more important to a man than being respected. If he doesn't feel respected he doesn't give love in the way a woman perceives love. If she doesn't feel loved, she doesn't give respect in the way a man needs to be respected. This is the essence of the battle of the sexes. It is a circle of insanity and we need to stop and get off the merry-go-round!

With Jack, he could not give me the love that I craved, and I could not respect him. He consistently trampled my needs as a beginning sailor, and I began to distrust him. With Didier, he needed my respect, and to him that meant he had to be in charge. The relationship would never work unless he felt that I respected him as the dominant partner, and he could not love me unless he held that position.

In the Bible, the Apostle Paul spoke to couples in a letter he wrote to the Ephesians. In it, he tells the women that they should *respect* their husbands, and he tells the men that they need to *love* their wives. So even when we look back thousands of years, these basic elements of *love and respect* have not changed. They will make or break any relationship, no matter where you live or play, whether you believe the Bible or not, or whether you are old-fashioned or modern in your views.

It may seem that I am oversimplifying the matter, but the formula really isn't that complicated. Give what you know your spouse needs first to have your own needs met in turn. If you know what your partner needs to be happy, give it. What we give comes back ten-fold. But if it's so simple, why do so many couples split up? Why do so many men end up single-handing the boats they bought with their wives and in which they were to embark on the greatest adventure of their lives?

I think people are often way too focused on themselves, and not enough on what is important to the one they love the most. If you are part of a couple, it's not just about you anymore. You really do need to take into account the other person that you share your life with. It is the difference between *me* and *us.* When you are too much into yourself, you will never be able to meet the needs of your partner. And when you don't meet the needs of your partner, there is the possibility that he will eventually go find someone else who will.

In the following pages, I will be presenting information I have gathered from years of making mistakes, doing research, and observing couples on boats. I am just presenting information, and what you do with it is up to you. The fact is that the health of all relationships (spouses, children, friends, and business associates) boils down to good communication, caring about others besides yourself, and a balance between give and take. When we spend more time taking than giving back, that imbalance is going to inevitably cause conflict, lack of satisfaction, and eventually someone is going to leave. You can't keep drinking from the same cup without refilling it. Eventually it will run empty.

When you listen to your partner he will tell you what is important to him. Too often we get wrapped up in ourselves and don't listen to what the other person is telling us. This is the first step on the path to divorce. If that doesn't sound too bad to you, believe me; the grass isn't greener on the other side. You take yourself with you to the other pasture, and if you don't change, you'll get the same result when you do the same thing with a different person.

The battle of the sexes is really about demanding what we want, while holding hostage what the other person needs. If a woman doesn't feel loved and adored she does not give respect. Then when a guy doesn't get respect he doesn't give that love. It is a Catch-22. Someone needs to stop the vicious cycle and say, "I will be the first to give what you need so that I can get what I need." When you love someone this should be easy to do. Someone has to take the first step. So who will it be?

SHOWING LOVE

What is the opposite of the selfishness I just described? A willingness to show love the way another person needs to see it demonstrated. There are a few basic ways that people in a relationship show love to each other. Each person has a preferred method. When you understand which method you use, and which your partner uses, you can make music together like a well-tuned orchestra. Just as there are various ways in which people learn, they also differ in how they feel or respond to love. Most people give what it is they want to receive. If you are even slightly observant you can figure this out. If someone is always showing up with a gift, he is really telling you that he would like gifts in return.

Some people need to have physical affection, and that doesn't just mean sex. It is also intimate touching like holding hands, putting your arm around that person, stroking her face or rubbing his back or feet. There are some people who feel loved when they receive things like flowers, gifts and trinkets. Another way of showing or receiving love is with the way you speak to your partner. Some people just need to hear those words, "I love you and I think you are special." They need to hear words that affirm, encourage, and build them up. It may not be important to you, but that is what he needs to hear. Still others need love to be shown by actions—completing a "honey-do" list might be better than chocolates! Sometimes time set apart for just the two of you can mean more to one than the other, but no gift or task will make up for a lack of dedicated attention. (For more about this topic, see Gary Chapman's *The Five Love Languages.*)

In order to begin to act in this way, two people have to be willing to think outside of themselves. If you know that the other person needs to feel loved in a certain way and you are only willing to show it in your way, will that person really feel loved? What are you willing to contribute to this relationship to see that it is successful? If you can't make it successful on land, how do you expect it to change when you are on a boat in the middle of an ocean, or on an island far from home? Before we move on, I'd like to say a few words to the ladies.

A WORD TO THE WIVES

In the book *For Women Only*, by Shaunti Feldhahn, seventy-one percent of men polled said they need to be the provider. Men are almost always thinking about their responsibility as a provider. It is a heavy weight they bear, even if the woman brings in an income, and even if she makes more money that he does.

I remember feeling the weight of responsibility when I sailed to the Bahamas on my boat. These were feelings that I never had when I sailed with my boyfriend in Seattle. I became very stressed by the feeling that I was the one responsible for the boat and other people's lives. I was constantly concerned about the boat and every little strange noise that I heard. I couldn't shake off all of those *what if's* in the back of my mind.

Guys have a lot of pressure on them that they don't talk about. A man doesn't talk about his fears and anxieties. He deals with his emotions by either disappearing into the cave or, if he cannot contain them, becoming unpleasant or angry. Very few men will come right out and say they are afraid.

In disagreements, men need to be able to save face. Ladies, you cannot embarrass or humiliate a man, especially in front of his peers, and then expect him to be friendly and cooperative or responsive emotionally or physically.

When a woman shows a man respect for his judgment and abilities, the guy will go to the extreme to please her. But when a woman does not show that respect, he will become defensive and angry. Women should not try and tell a guy what to do in areas in which she does not have expertise. For example, if you don't know anything about engines, don't try and tell him how to fix one. The way we present information can sometimes sound like disrespect. Even if he isn't that knowledgeable about engines, don't embarrass him by telling others, especially other men. Don't give the impression that he is incapable of fixing the problem.

Guys are problem solvers and they ask for help in a different ways than women do. Men don't want to be reminded of their shortcomings. Who does? So find those things that you can appreciate in each other instead of always pointing out those things that are lacking.

ON THE BOAT

How does all of this play out on a boat? If you are having problems in your relationship to begin with, buying a boat and going cruising with someone will not help you to "get away from it all"—it will actually bring dysfunction into greater focus in the small and sometimes stressful environment of a boat. If, for example, you find yourselves having the same argument over and over again, it is probably because you have underlying conflict. That problem will never go away until the conflict is resolved. Going cruising will simply bring the conflict to the surface, and usually during a moment of crisis. Living on a boat can test even the best of marriages, requiring a great deal of grace and understanding from both partners, but it can bring conflict to a boiling point for couples that are already struggling. How can they resolve this conflict?

The way to resolve it is to sit down and really listen to what is being

said, and find the common ground on which both of you can be happy. What is at the bottom of the conflict? Is it more her discomfort with the whole cruising dream, rather than dissatisfaction with him personally? For example, she may not want to cruise twelve months out of the year, but she could possibly be talked into cruising for half of the year. Maybe she doesn't want to miss seeing the grandbabies grow up. Six months is better than nothing, right? Find a compromise to please each other. Maybe she just needs to be willing to trust him and give it a try, to see what it is all about.

Perhaps the conflict is about the endless tinkering he does on the boat. Having her home always in a state of confusion or her salon table looking like a tool bench might put a woman off. But if she respects him and tries to understand where he is coming from, she will be willing to put up with a lot more. When men feel respected and appreciated for the efforts they make to protect their partners and to give them comfort and safety, they will try harder to please women. His working on the boat is his way of showing that he cares. He can't help wanting to protect and provide, he is hard-wired to do so. How she responds to him can change the whole equation when it comes to the atmosphere inside the boat.

Or maybe he is insensitive to his wife's fear when they're out on the water. The amount of wind, waves and heel are all factors that can make or break the deal for a couple. Women need to feel loved and adored. If guys respect a woman's comfort level and take a reef when the boat is heeled more than she likes, it will make her feel like he cares about what is important to her; the underlying message is "I love you and I would rather see you happy and by my side, than to scare you or disregard your feelings." If they are in cruising mode, time should never be a deciding factor. An extra day in the anchorage, waiting out the stronger winds and allowing the seas to settle down a little more can make a huge difference in the comfort of the crew on the way to the next destination. Some couples make a pact that unless they are in complete agreement, they won't pull the anchor up. Consensus—what a concept! It's even better than compromise.

These are just a few examples of how the need for love and respect surface in a relationship at sea. When couples try to see each other's point of view and work toward agreement or compromise, communicating love and respect, their needs are being met and there is harmony.

COMPROMISE AND MUTUAL RESPECT

After becoming a single-hander by choice, I spent a lot of time talking to other cruising couples who had been sailing successfully together for years, and asking how they made it work. The one thing I heard repeated over and over was that they had maintained mutual respect, with both people acknowledging the other's individual needs and comfort levels.

Respect is mandatory and it is a two-way street. Our motives for doing things are different. He is motivated by adventure, and she by safety and security. While she needs to respect his adventuresome spirit, he must yield a bit so she can feel comfortable and safe. The bottom line is that women need to be appreciated, understood, and allowed to talk about their feelings. For men to feel loved and appreciated, they need to be respected and trusted. When each has their "love tank" filled up with what is important to them, then there is an abundance of love to go around. Their tanks will be over-flowing.

So next time you think, "What about me?" Ask yourself, "How much did I contribute to my partner's tank?" Ask how you have met your partner's needs, wants, and desires. If you have not been putting in your share, then you cannot demand to take out more. It's not about keeping score, but about making a concerted effort to contribute to the other's well-being. If you have given then you can ask for a share. If both set out with the same goal, it's a win-win situation.

Think of it like contributing your financial funds toward the cruising kitty. You both keep putting your change into the savings account. Now there is plenty, so you both can enjoy the fruits of your labor. It is the same with giving and taking love. If the bank account is empty there is nothing to take. Keep each other's bank account full!

Give each other affirmation when your needs are met. Don't focus on what is still lacking, but emphasize the successes. Gratitude encourages

positive change, success breeds success.

CB

The next chapter is full of suggestions on how to show love and respect on a boat and how to meet each others' needs. Remember, this is a two-way street. Don't go to your partner and say, "Look, here it is in black and white. You need to do this!" Instead, say, "Let's look at this together to see what works for us. What is it that we may have been missing?" Use the topics as a springboard for discussion. It can help resolve issues you may already have, helping you to clear the air and start fresh. I wish you the best.

Two on a Boat How to Keep it Afloat

FOURTEEN

Strategies for Sailing
Together in Harmony

*You can keep doing what you have been doing with the same
results or you can try something new and get better results.*

SUGGESTED DO'S AND DON'TS FOR BOTH GENDERS

This chapter contains suggestions and ideas for couples who want to
create harmony aboard a boat. As you can see in the picture, Harmony
is a real place, but it can also exist anywhere, on land or at sea. Some
of the suggestions are no-brainers and are easy to accomplish. Others
may take a bit more work and dedication. But the rewards of having
peace and happiness on your boat and in your
relationship will be well worth the effort.

DON'T SCARE YOUR PARTNER

Terrifying a person does not impress them.
The only thing it will accomplish is send them
in the opposite direction. If you want to become a single-hander, this
is a guaranteed way to do it. I know too many married men who are
single-handing because they just didn't get this! Maybe they want to sail
alone. I don't know.

If you are a single guy wondering why you can't get the girls to come back for a second sail, start looking internally, not externally. It's not them, it's you.

Respect never goes out of style and it works both ways. Treating someone the way you want to be treated, with the utmost care and respect, goes a long way.

MAKE SURE THERE IS TWO-WAY COMMUNICATION

Don't Ass-U-Me anything! You can avoid a whole lot of arguments, yelling and regrets by never assuming anything.

This is worth repeating; make sure there is always two-way communication. A grunt, a head nod, a hand signal are all acceptable, and complete the two-way path of communication. However, keep in mind that a non-verbal response is only effective if the other person can see you.

USE NON-VERBAL COMMUNICATION

Make sure that you agree on the hand signals. You cannot use the same signal for "look over there" as "go over there". Using hand signals and responses is the same as above; there should always be a *two-way* communication. Visual contact is required.

Also, eliminate the negative non-verbal communication, such as hand and facial expressions. If you don't like someone saying or doing it to you, then don't do it to anyone else.

MAKE ONLY ONE ASSUMPTION

If you don't get an answer, you can assume the person did NOT hear you! I really want everyone to get this, but guys especially. One word works! "OK" or "Got it!" Any little thing! You will find half of the arguments will go away when she gets that tiny little verbal acknowledgement.

SHARE THE THOUGHT PROCESS

Keep the dialog open. Guys, discuss with her what is going on in your mind. Try to talk through your decision-making, play-by-play. Help your partner to understand your thought process so she can learn to do the same. Sometimes it's about helping her to have more confidence in you and your abilities. It doesn't mean you have to do this all the time. I don't have to ask the ladies to do this because they do it automatically! But, ladies, you can help him by asking specific questions when you need clarification.

TRUST YOUR PARTNER'S ABILITIES

Don't always doubt and question your partner's decisions. For ladies, this comes across as lack of respect for a man. For guys, she needs the whole picture for assurance that everything is okay. When you make decisions together a lot of this problem goes away.

The more you learn, the less you have to question. So make sure you know things for yourself, by learning navigation and other skills.

When I was in the Bahamas I would plug all the waypoints along my route into the GPS. I had played with this handheld GPS and learned how to use it. Didier did not spend time learning how to use the GPS because he preferred the paper chart method. He would get frustrated and doubt that the GPS headings were correct. He hadn't used the equipment enough, nor had he looked at what I had done with the charts. So I told him to check my work and he started looking at the charts and comparing everything I did. Once he saw it and understood it, we were both in agreement.

I did not feel that he didn't trust me or doubted my ability, but just that he didn't understand what I was doing. He didn't have the whole picture. I put my ego aside and helped him to learn how to use the equipment, rather than taking it as a criticism of my abilities.

DON'T WAIT UNTIL THE LAST MINUTE TO DO SOMETHING

Sailing shouldn't have to feel like a fire drill to the crew. Too often, someone new to sailing is sitting on the boat just enjoying the scenery, the breeze, maybe the sight of dolphins in the distance and that is about all that is running though his mind. He or she may have no idea of potential hazards. To suddenly hear, "We need to Tack NOW!" is a frightening situation.

For someone who really doesn't know what is going on, it feels like a crisis. Even though you told him or her about the jib sheet, their brain shuts down and they go into overload. They panic and feel as if something really bad is about to happen.

To most people who are experienced sailors, they have either forgotten or have no idea what this feels like to the other person. It is scary for the person who doesn't understand, even though you may feel totally in control. Have a little compassion for that less-experienced person.

HOLD DEBRIEFING SESSIONS

When problems happen, and they WILL, you should always have a debriefing session AFTER the boat is secure and safe. Please, please, please make it an opportunity for a learning lesson rather than an argument. I hate to admit it, but all of my confidence as a sailor, captain, and instructor has come from problems and mistakes. Yes, I have made many mistakes.

It is ridiculous that we always want to blame and get upset with each other when things don't work out perfectly. Are you forgetting that we do not live in a perfect world? Getting irritated with someone is not going to change what happened. Arguments and blame only cause hurt feelings between two people. It can allow resentment to creep in. Resentments start compounding into doubt in the other person's love, and eventually you just don't want to be with someone who is going to doubt you or argue with you all the time. And this goes both ways.

I have become the instructor to the instructors' wives. I have had quite a few wives of sailing instructors attend my classes over the last few years. This proves that most husbands cannot teach their wives — even professionals. One particular wife recently told me how she would get angry with her husband and a lot of the arguments were out of her own ignorance. Because she didn't understand, she would doubt him.

After taking the classes and understanding all the things that he was doing and why he was doing them, she developed a greater respect and appreciation for her husband. Now she looks at him with new eyes and realizes that she was contributing to the problem because she didn't understand. They say knowledge is power, and I say, *understanding brings peace.*

ALWAYS FORGIVE EACH OTHER

Don't ever go to bed angry at each other, especially not over something as insignificant as sailing. (In comparison to the marriage, sailing is trivial.) Also, forgiving means choosing *not* to bring the old resentments into a future argument. I know one couple who actually says the words to each other after a disagreement, "I'm sorry," and "I forgive you." If the magic words are uttered, then that disagreement is not allowed to be brought up *ever* again as an example of someone's shortcomings. This preventative maintenance means that any new conflict that arises is not simply a re-hashing of old resentments. This couple clears the air and is able to move toward resolution very quickly. Note that the offended person doesn't say, "That's okay." There is acknowledgment of wrongdoing in forgiveness, but also freedom.

Try to take positive lessons from trying situations. Always ask yourself, what can I learn from this? How can I be a better person, sailor, etc?

ALLOW TIME FOR THE LEARNING CURVE

Don't expect perfection from those less experienced than you are.

Don't ask anyone new to sailing or boating to do something unless you explain the process first. That way they understand the final outcome or the desired result. Telling someone to "just pull on that line," is not enough information. How hard should they pull? How much should they pull? What is going to happen when they pull that line? Does it have a proper name? Use that proper name. Be more specific and detailed.

Be kind to any guests aboard, particularly when they lack experience or knowledge. This goes both ways for guys and gals.

LADIES, DEFINE YOUR FEARS AND CONCERNS

You are responsible for speaking up regarding your concerns or confusion. Guys, sometimes just validating those feelings and fears and showing respect can help minimize them.

Both people have a responsibility in this. She first needs to identify the problem, and then the two of you can work together to find the solution. Because women are verbal processors, they need to brainstorm out loud to discover the issues that are causing dissonance. The next step is to make an active effort to address the fears. Take classes, find other women to network with, etc. *Don't just live in the mud puddle, get out and wash yourself off.*

CURB THE FOUL LANGUAGE

Better yet, don't use foul language at all. Try talking nicely to each other. This goes both ways. Eliminate the four letter words completely. There is no excuse for it! Talking does not include cussing, yelling, or derogatory comments, even if someone messes up. Show the respect you want in return.

ESTABLISH GROUND RULES FOR CONFLICT

Conflict is a reality in any relationship, but it doesn't have to be ugly.

A disagreement is just that: two people who don't agree. A disagreement does not have to become a fight. Just like a game of chess has rules, agree on rules for conflict. For example, you might decide on a 15-minute cooling-off period if someone loses his temper, or to never go to bed angry, or to never re-hash an old argument. Be creative, but once you make the rules, stick to them and hold each other accountable.

RESPECT YOUR PARTNER'S COMFORT LEVEL

Don't heel the boat so much if it makes her nervous. It isn't efficient anyway! More than 15 degrees of heel increases the boat's leeway. Ease the main sheet or traveler, or take a reef to keep the boat under control. This is even more important if you are sailing short-handed and/or at night. It's amazing how such a simple thing can ease the stress of sailing when you are alone on deck at night.

Slowing the boat down results in slightly longer passages, but the joy of sailing is about the journey, not killing yourself to get there. As an added benefit, you can rest easy and have peace of mind when leaving your partner at the helm if you know the boat is not going to be over-powered. She will be more willing to stand a watch alone if she feels the boat is under control for her. It works for both of you.

Respect is mandatory! Every person has a different comfort level when it comes to the strength of the wind, height of the seas, and the angle of the boat's heel. You may not go as fast, and you may take a little longer to get there, but isn't it worth the peace and happiness for your partner?

Women are less willing to go out again, or go the distance, when their comfort level is not respected. I have found that for most women their comfort level will increase with training, understanding, and good experiences.

TAKE THE TIME TO LEARN HOW TO SAIL TOGETHER

Guys, even if you know how to sail, you can be in the class as a support for her. It never hurts to hear the information more than once. You might actually learn a thing or two, plus how to work better together as a team. Who would object to spending some time on the water? Besides, it's fun.

HELP THOSE WHO DON'T HAVE PHYSICAL STRENGTH

If the wind is too strong, or if the crew is short on upper body strength, the helmsman can help by pinching the boat up into the wind. The sails luff momentarily, making it easier for the crew to finish sheeting in the sail. So *what if* the sail luffs a little bit. You are not racing, remember?

SPEAK IN A STANDARD LANGUAGE

People need to learn the language before they can communicate effectively. The language of sailing is gibberish to a landlubber. This includes the standard language for points of sail, commands and responses, etc. You can find them on the back of the *Sailing Wind Wheel*. A good example is the words, "fall off." Landlubbers might think you are asking them to fall off the boat when you are really telling them to fall off the wind. Allow new people time to learn, and always use correct terms.

Whether you are sailing on an Americas Cup boat or out cruising in your own boat, the language needs to be the same. You should be able to go from boat to boat and speak the same language. Don't start making up new words, like a tight reach when you mean a close haul, or a deep beam reach for a broad reach. Nobody understands that. It just confuses people more. Stick to the right names.

FIND A BALANCE WHEN IT COMES TO INFORMATION

Don't overload someone new to sailing with too much explanation in the beginning. You don't always have to provide all the details in the beginning. Keep it simple, but complete. Not everyone needs the long

version right away. If more explanation is needed, you can always refer to the *Annapolis Book of Seamanship*. That's why it was written.

DESIGNATE THE CAPTAIN-OF-THE-DAY

Maritime Law states there must always be a designated Skipper aboard. Legally, there must be one person who is ultimately responsible for the boat. But take turns. By taking turns both partners are equally learning how to make good decisions. When a woman is learning, she is apt to state her command more like a question. Don't take it that she doesn't know the right answer. Give her the kudos for making the right decision, and if you don't agree explain why. Again, it is an opportunity to learn not to be put down. She will ask less when she feels more confident.

AGREE TO DISAGREE

When the boat is in a crisis you may not agree on how to handle the problem. Someone has to make a decision, and the time you spend arguing can cause things to go from bad to worse. The time to disagree is not in the middle of an emergency.

The final decision belongs to the person who is also legally liable for every person on that boat. That is why everyone aboard is required to obey the skipper. It is still legally considered an act of mutiny when someone disobeys the skipper.

When things go wrong, decisions need to be made quickly and there is not always time for explanations or reasoning. That time could end up a matter of life or death.

As you saw in previous chapters, there are always a variety of ways to handle a problem. The time to discuss other options is when the boat is safe. It's better to review the lesson later than to cause problems and arguments.

HAVE A BACKUP PLAN

Always have a plan "A", and a backup plan "B", for things like docking and anchoring. It doesn't hurt to have a "C" either. This will save a lot of heartache when things start going wrong. I can't tell you how often things can go wrong when leaving the dock or returning to the dock. When you understand the dynamics of the boat, its inherent tendencies, and how the boat is going to be affected by the wind and the current, you can plan and prepare a head of time with an alternate plan. Notice, this is a verbal discussion.

Almost every time I teach people on their own boats, the first thing I do is change dock lines to set them up for success. There are many ways you can set up your own slip to make it almost dummy proof. What a pleasure to go sailing when the docking experience is not a crisis every time.

REMEMBER THE KISS METHOD

Everything on a boat is designed to be easy. Take one step at a time. Don't try to do too many things at once. *Keep It Simple, Sweetheart* and remember, no one is stupid when they are learning!

DIVIDE AND CONQUER

The "Pink" duties and "Blue" duties should not mean that she is the galley wench and he is the skipper. Each person needs to be proficient in all aspects onboard instead of always assuming the same responsibilities. She doesn't always need to cook, and he doesn't always need to be at the helm docking the boat.

Take turns learning and knowing all the jobs on the boat. Find out your strengths and weaknesses. Don't just do the things you are good at. If you are not good at docking, go learn how to dock!

At the same time, a good division of labor can make a boat run like clockwork. The secret is to agree on *who* is going to do *what*, and *when*,

then stick to it.

ALLOW PERSONAL SPACE

Allow your partner his personal space. Even if you've been married twenty-five years, it is different when you are on a small boat and living 24/7 with that person. We all have our routines and idiosyncrasies and in small spaces those habits can become irritants.

One couple I met in the Bahamas were opposites with their sleep habits. She liked to stay up at night reading, and he would go to bed early. He loved being up early to watch the sunrises. It was his chance to get the alone time he needed. It worked for both of them without the expectation that one or the other would have to change their habits.

DON'T BE A KNOW-IT-ALL

Those who think they know it all are usually the fools, or make fools of themselves. Mother Nature can be brutal to those who think they can outsmart her. Humility goes a long way on the big blue ocean. There is always room to grow in knowledge and ability on the sea. Always endeavor to be learning and growing.

DON'T HAVE UNREALISTIC EXPECTATIONS

Demonstrate a task first, and ask if the person understands, before expecting them to do themselves. It is ridiculous to say, "pull on that halyard" when someone is may not even know what a halyard is. It's like asking for the flubber. It's just plain gibberish to the person with whom you are speaking. If it causes the person to become embarrassed, he may be wary of even participating in the future.

DON'T BELITTLE ANYONE

When someone doesn't understand what you are saying, it means you need to find a different way to say it. Raising your voice or speaking in a condescending manner does not make people comprehend the information. You must find a different way of conveying what you what. It's about you being clear and not expecting others to read your mind.

DON'T GET ANGRY

Don't get angry when your partner does things differently. Embrace each other's differences. Don't try to change people. People don't change easily. You have one of two choices; either accept those traits, or leave. A leopard doesn't change his spots.

ACCEPT THAT YOUR PARTNER PROCESSES THINGS DIFFERENTLY

She needs to talk about the same thing repeatedly to process and learn. Her verbally processing is an opportunity to guide her if she is not getting something correct. Guidance should be done without making judgment on her ability to learn or to grasp the information. We all learn at different paces.

He needs to go "into the cave." Stop trying to get him to talk. Don't ask a guy, "What are you thinking?" Don't think that he is upset at you because he needs to go into the cave for a while. Allow him to do his processing, and then he will share his conclusions. Don't take it personally, or think that something negative is going on when he is simply mulling things over to himself. Ultimately, you both should come together and share your conclusions.

DON'T PLAY THE BLAME GAME

Let go of egos when things go wrong. Don't blame others or worse,

216

blame yourself, when things don't work the way you thought they would or should.

I have to admit that I do allow a single night to beat myself up when things go wrong. I review it over and over in my mind until I come up with a solution, so that I can be better prepared for the next time. I have both gained confidence in my skills as a result, and responded better in subsequent similar situations when they arose. In some cases, I found a way to avoid the situation so that I didn't have to experience it again.

TRUST YOUR GUT INSTINCTS

Guys think women are usually overreacting when she says, "I have a bad feeling," and can't say exactly why. Guys usually ignore their own nagging instincts. Every single time that I ignore those instincts, I end up regretting it.

There have been so many times when I have looked at the weather and told my students that it was not a good idea to go, but because they started complaining, I would give in and agree. In one instance a couple insisted even after I repeatedly told the couple that the weather would be bad. When we got caught in the bad weather and she got scared and seasick, with whom do you think they were upset?

You can learn it the hard way, or take it from me. And remember guys, if you don't listen to her, you may be hearing those dreaded words, "I told you so!"

DON'T LET EXHAUSTION CAUSE PROBLEMS

I can't tell you how many times I have seen people get into petty arguments after doing the overnight trip to the Bahamas. Usually, when there are just two people aboard. You don't get much sleep when you are standing four hour watches. Even when you are off-watch, if you feel responsible for the boat you will wake up to every unusual noise or motion.

It's easy to understand how people with sleep deprivation will become cranky, irritable, and edgy. Silly and petty little arguments occur when people are tired. Don't let it happen, or when it does, recognize it for what it is and quickly make amends.

The worst case is when you both have to stay up because the winds and waves are too strong, or you are caught in a storm. People make bad decisions when they are exhausted. Heave-to if you are far enough offshore, take shorter watches, or bring more crew. Whatever it takes to make sure everyone is well-rested and safe.

DON'T CONFUSE CRUISING WITH RACING

People who are racers and speed demons need to find a way to satisfy their need for exhilaration separate from cruising with their spouses. Do your racing on the racecourse, but when cruising please shift down to low gear for those in your life who like the relaxed casual sailing mode.

STAY FLEXIBLE

Sailing boils down to respect, communication, and being flexible. Be flexible in the way you think and the way you respond. Be ready to change the plan when things don't work as expected. Sailing is about constantly adapting to a changing environment of wind and waves. You should always to be ready to change the plan when the environment does. Change is the only constant. Remember, *that which does not bend will break*. Being flexible means that you may bend, but you will recover.

⚃

I'm sure I could keep adding to the list but you get the idea. Sailing is such a great metaphor for life. You can relate so many things back to sailing.

I hope that seeing life through your partner's eyes will help each of you enjoy and appreciate each other even more than you did when you first decided to embark on your journey together. If you are single and looking to find a partner for life or a partner to sail with, I hope that these ideas and suggestions will help you to keep your mind and eyes open to possibilities, and to better appreciate those with whom you sail, whether for a day or a lifetime.

Two on a Boat How to Keep it Afloat

Fifteen

Women's Resources

Women naturally understand what women need, so it makes sense to go to a woman for help with female needs. It is not to say that men cannot be just as good at teaching women, just that women have an invisible connection.

TEN REASONS TO TAKE THE STEP

By now I think you know the value and importance of having resources for women sailors, and opportunities for them to learn from other women. Women teaching women works well because the instructor can better relate to her students and is sympathetic to what her students need.

Eight out of ten of my classes are actually booked by husbands and boyfriends. I truly appreciate and admire those men because they already understand that their wives and girlfriends need something he doesn't know how to give. They also realize that when her needs are met, he will get what he wishes, too.

With most of the couples that I have taught over the last five years, the most common scenario has been for me to have conversations with the husband about the sailing classes. It is his dream to go sailing, but his wife is hesitant. He knows he needs to help her overcome her fears, but he doesn't know what practical steps to take. She is reserved, reluctant or even recalcitrant!

Women are more willing to come and learn once they hear that the class is with a female captain. They feel that a woman can better relate, and won't yell at them or make them feel stupid. Often when they read my background information, they know we have something in common and I understand where they are coming from.

Once I uncover a woman's reservations, it is easy to help her become a confident sailor. There is nothing more empowering for a woman than being at the helm docking the boat. This is the one thing she doesn't believe that she can ever do. So once I prove to a woman that she can do it, there is no stopping her. I love to see women grow in confidence on the boat. And I know for a fact that there isn't a woman out there who cannot learn and become as proficient as her partner. I learned to single-hand in order to be a good mate. I am not out to sail the seven seas alone!

Private classes for couples are growing in popularity, and there are now many accomplished women captains and instructors who teach sailing all over the country. There is no reason why you cannot find a female captain wherever you live or desire to sail.

Here are ten things that may help motivate you to consider taking some kind of training. If you ever want to move into a place of confidence, a place of growing and experiencing new things with your spouse, take a class. If you ever want to escape that place of *F-E-A-R* (remember the acronym from chapter four?) take steps to become proficient.

1. You will finally understand the language everyone else is speaking on the boat. You will be able to respond appropriately, rather than feeling fearful, confused, or just doing what you are told.

2. You will learn proper communication with all the correct commands and responses. You will know what they mean and why we use them.

3. You will understand the wind and how to properly trim the sails for optimal performance.

4. You will know how to keep the boat at your comfort level and under control at all times.

5. You will know how to handle the boat when the wind shifts.

6. You will know where you are and where you are going, even if all the instruments malfunction.

7. You will be able to determine when other boats may be a cause for concern how to properly react to situations rather than panic.

8. You will be able to steer the boat and know how to dock it confidently.

9. You will know how to do M.O.B. maneuvers both under power and under sail. You will be able to have confidence that you can save someone's life if they fall overboard.

10. You will be able to overcome fears of things like jibing or handling the boat in a storm.

WOMEN SAILING CONNECTION BY WOMEN FOR WOMEN

The Women Sailing Connection website (www.womensailing. com) is full of women captains and instructors throughout the U.S. and Canada. The website is always being updated with new captains, instructors, classes, and resources. The goal is for women and couples to find a class that is right for them. This doesn't just have to be a female instructor. If the organization supports women and couples you will find it here.

As of the writing of this book, website membership is free. When you become a member, you can be notified of the various women's programs being offered around the country, as well as special online offers for training, classes, clinics, etc.

There are annual women's programs that provide a variety of classes and clinics from novice to racing in the same weekend. You can improve your M.O.B. skills and learn to tie knots. You can pick several different classes throughout the day. On the East Coast there is an annual Women's Conference held in Massachusetts, and in California there is a two day Women's Seminar that has been going for many years now. Out in the Pacific Northwest, there is an annual Women's Seminar held in February. These are just some of the clinics you can find through the website.

You can find a captain in your area or the area you would like to sail, and learn a little bit about them. For women, it is very important to know something about a captain or instructor and find a commonality, or just have some idea of what you're getting into before you spend the time, effort and money.

It's not all work; there are places to go just for fun to use your skills in exotic places and my goal is to keep adding classes like catamaran training. There are, of course, many instructors and resources for couples. You can search for women instructors by location or by the type of class you are looking for.

The best thing is that you can know before you go. Some schools put you with whoever is on the schedule. It may not be the right person for you, and you may not get the *TLC* you need. Most schools will not specify who the instructor will be, nor provide you with their background, experience, or reputation. Now you don't have to risk ending up with a Captain Bligh. You can read all about the backgrounds of the captains and instructors ahead of time. This makes it easy to find someone with whom you can connect. You will know the type of person with whom you will be sailing, so you can feel as if you already know the instructor before you even get there.

You will also find some new online seminars that I am putting together. See the back for more information.

TWO SUCCESS STORIES

I initially met **EARLENE** when she took my classes, but she has since become a very good friend of mine. She had contacted me several years before she actually took her classes with me. Many people

investigate taking sailing classes, but don't follow through for one reason or another. For Earlene, she finally decided to take the sailing classes as a memorial to her husband who had recently passed away.

After her first two days of sailing lessons, she told me that she was blown away at what she had learned, and how she regretted not following through years ago when she had first contacted me, because it would have changed everything that happened on the boat between her and her husband.

Her husband told her, like many husbands do, "You don't need to take sailing lessons, I'll teach you." But as with me, Earlene, and many other women, it never happens. She fell into the typical scenario where she just did what she was told, because she just didn't understand what was going on or how to do things.

Earlene's story is representative of so many others. Too many women live with their fears rather than making the decision to finally take the lessons and learn to sail confidently. You are ultimately responsible for your own experience; you can't blame your husband forever.

I'm proud to say that Earlene has become a very confident and capable sailor. She purchased a little twenty-three foot O'Day, and loves her little boat. She has also met Bill, who lives aboard his fifty-foot boat. The experience she now shares with Bill is very different because she is  enjoying the sailing, and she is able to be a part of all that is going on when they sail together. She is no longer just a passenger, but a full, confident participant. She writes:

> When I was first learning to sail, I was intimidated by big boats with big sails and lots of gadgets with names that made no sense to me. I had no confidence in my skills and neither did my husband. As a result, I became nothing more than a human autopilot. I'd position myself behind the wheel and follow his directions. If I did the wrong thing, or didn't react quickly enough to confusing commands, I got yelled at. Many pleasant

afternoons of sailing ended with me in tears saying, "Don't yell at me" and my husband responding, "I'm not YELLING!" I loved being on the water, but this was not fun. After he passed away, I decided to find an instructor who would take the confusion out of sailing and help me gain the confidence I needed. An online search brought me to Captain Josie. What a difference she made!! With her "no yelling" approach to teaching and clear instructions, I was allowed to make mistakes and ask question after question, without feeling like I was stupid. In just one afternoon on the water with Captain Josie, I learned more than I had in my previous four years of sailing experience. Since then, I have earned 3 certifications and I now have the skills I need to sail confidently, not only as an able crew member, but to single-hand my boat.

ROSEANNE is another woman whose story to which I believe many women will be able to relate. Roseanne was not interested in having anything to do with any part of sailing the boat. She was just going

along for the ride, and I think even that was with reluctance sometimes.

Roseanne and her husband wanted to do more than just day sails, but they couldn't because of docking issues. She was not able to jump off the boat because of a physical limitation. If they were going to do any traveling where they would dock at distant ports, she would have to learn to be the helmsman and dock the boat.

Roseanne also didn't like the boat to heel over, so her husband would always sail with the main sheet in hand, ready to make adjustments to keep the boat level. What a great guy!

One day during a sailing lesson with a group of women that included Roseanne, the wind kicked up enough that I had to take a reef. I noticed how much the boat was heeling and I knew a couple of the women were uncomfortable with this. I will never forget when I looked over at Roseanne at the helm and asked, "Are you okay?" She said, "Yes, why?" I said, "Look how much the boat is heeling." She replied, "I didn't even notice." Wow—how things change when we gain our confidence.

❧

I could tell you many stories like this. Many of these women I am proud to consider more than just students, but also friends. There is nothing more rewarding than to see women blossom aboard the boat. I truly believe that every woman can become confident and competent in all tasks aboard a boat. (If you want to read more comments by past students log on to www.acss.bz.)

I will leave you with this thought. When you are old and telling stories to your grandchildren and great grandchildren, will you be telling them stories of your adventures and inspiring them? Or will you be reminded of what you wish you had done and filled with regrets instead?

Be afraid, but do it anyway. Knowledge is power, and by learning how to handle your boat you will overcome most of what is holding you back from achieving your goals or your husband's dreams. Do it for yourself as well as for him. Know that you are able to do anything that you put your mind to. I believe in you.

May the Lord, bless you and keep you, and may His light shine upon you and give you peace, and keep you safe as you travel through life on and off the oceans blue.

Suggested additional reading for women on the water:

Cantrell, Debra Ann, *Changing Course – A Woman's Guide to Choosing the Cruising Life,* International Marine/McGraw-Hill, 2004

Copeland, Liza, *Cruising for Cowards,* Romany Publishing, 2008

Giesemann, Suzanne, *It's Your Boat Too,* Paradise Cay Publications, 2006

Two on a Boat How to Keep it Afloat

Jessie, Diana, *The Cruising Woman's Advisor: How to Prepare for the Voyaging Life,* International Marine/McGraw-Hill, 1997

Pardey, Lin & Larry, *The Self-Sufficient Sailor,* Pardey Books, 1997

Shard, Paul and Sheryl, *Sail Away! A Guide to Outfitting and Provisioning for Cruising,* Pelagic Press, 1998

Trefethen, Jim, *Cruising Life, How to set sail within five years and live well and adventurously, even if you don't have a boat yet.* McGraw Hill, 1999

On the next pages are pictures of past students between 2004-2009, they are not in any particular order and represent only a small group of students from over the years. I apologize for leaving anyone out it was not intentional. You can read their comments about their class at www.acss.bz

Some classes are on my boat, others were taught on their boat. Everyone has a different goal and a different story. . . Most of my students have truely become friends.

TWO ON A BOAT HOW TO KEEP IT AFLOAT

Two on a Boat How to Keep it Afloat

Two on a Boat How to Keep it Afloat

Bibliography

Brizendine, Louann, MD, The Female Brain, Morgan Road Books, 2006

Chapman, Gary, The Five Love Languages, How to Express Heartfelt Commitment to Your Mate, Northfield Publishing, 1992, 1995

Chesneau, Lee and Li Chen, MA, Heavy Weather Avoidance and Route Design, Paradise Cay Publications, 2008

Eggerichs, Emerson Dr., Love & Respect. The love she most desires, the respect he desperately needs. Integrity Publishers, Brentwood, TN, 2004

Feldhahn, Shaunti and Jeff, For Men Only, Multnomah Books, 2006

Feldhahn, Shaunti, For Women Only, Multnomah Books, 2004

Gray, John, PhD. Men Are From Mars, Women Are From Venus. Harper Collins, New York, 1992.

Guzzewell, John, Trekka Round the World. Revised 1998

Legato, Marianne, MD, Why Men Never Remember and Women Never Forget

Longo, Richard, Sea Episodes of a Sailor, Author House, 2005 (In loving memory of my father, 1928-2005)

Moore, Denton R., Gentlemen Never Sail to Weather, The Story of an Accidental Odyssey, 1993

Nestor, Gregg, Twenty Affordable Sailboats to Take You Anywhere, Paradise Cay Publications, Inc. 2007

Quinn, Eileen, Lyrics from the CD, No Significant Features.

Rau, Tom, Boat Smart Chronicles, Seaworthy Publications, 2006

Tannen, Deborah. You Just Don't Understand! Women and Men in Conversation. Harper Collins, New York, 2001

ABOUT CAPTAIN JOSIE LONGO

Josie, received her ATA Legal Assistant degree in 1984 and worked as a Paralegal for over a decade, in Seattle, Washington. She has worked in complex litigations and assisted on the Washington Nuclear Power Plant, litigation and the MGM Fire litigation. She has also worked in tax law, medical malpractice and personal injury law. She was also a Limited Practice Officer, which means that she was sworn in by the State Supreme Court of the Sate of Washington, as a limited practice attorney, within the limited scope of Real Estate. This is a glorified name for an escrow closer.

She owned her own fitness business as a personal trainer and step aerobics instructor. She was certified with the American College of Sports Medicine, which is equivalent to a Bachelors degree in Physiology and Kinesiology.

Josie got her start on sailboats in 1991, in the Pacific Northwest. She sailed throughout Puget Sound, the San Juan Islands and as far north as the Canadian inside passage to Desolation Sound.

In 1996 she moved to Florida and made multiple passages to the Bahamas with the Gulfstream Sailing Club, on Memorial and Labor Day weekends for four years. She also made several passages on her own boat including single-handing throughout the Exuma's in the winter of 2000.

Captain Josie holds a USCG 50 GT Masters License and has been teaching private classes for couples since 2003. She lived aboard her 28' O'day for 7 years, in the Saint Petersburg area. She made two ocean passages with 10,000+ ocean miles. In 2001, she sailed on 162' Mega Yacht Michaela Rose, from Antigua to Copenhagen and then spent several weeks sailing in Corfu, Greece on a 50 foot catamaran. In 2002 she sailed the 70' aluminum cutter, Maya, from Seattle, Washington to Nuka Hiva in the French Polynesia.

She has a diverse sailing resume which includes sailing in New Zealand, Maine, all of the Florida Keys, San Diego, the BVI, and completed a circumnavigation around the DelMaVa Peninsula.

Her mission in teaching has always been to help women gain their confidence, couples to learn to live and play together without the yelling and guide people in the right direction for their personal goals whether it is owning a boat, cruising, chartering, fractional ownership or living aboard. Since she has done all of them she can relate from experience and can provide practical advise giving the pros and cons for each option.

OTHER BOOKS BY CAPTAIN JOSIE LONGO

THE SAILING WIND WHEEL & 2X2 MICRO METHOD

In chapter 10 Captain Josie talks about her invention, the **Sailing Wind Wheel.** This is the only hands-on visual and interactive, and 3-dimensional teaching tool. You can see it on the website www.sailingwindwheel.com

Her companion-training manual th**e *2x2 Micro Method*** was designed to compliment the Sailing Wind Wheel. All the components of sailing have been broken down into it's simplest of forms and then built back up to make learning and understanding the basics of sailing a breeze.

Between the Sailing Wind Wheel, which is very visual and interactive, and the 2x2 Micro Method manual people, male and female, adults and children, will find they can become instant naturals on the water with this method of learning.

Many people who have claimed they could never understand the wind are saying that finally the light came on and they claim this method was so easy they didn't understand why it took so long to get it in the first place.

Everything in the manual is in full color. You can see a demonstration of the Sailing Wind Wheel on the Internet. And stays in line with her philosophy: Keep It Simple Sweetheart!

 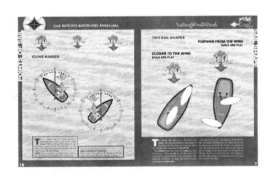

LIVE ONLINE TRAINING SESSIONS

Captain Josie teaches, "*Understanding the Wind*" via live online training sessions. You can learn the basics of sailing with her live, from the comfort of your own home at a time that works for you.

Go to sailingwindwheel.com/disc for a 10% discount plus receive a 10% discount with Captain Josie's new online live training seminar with the code: 2OB. (You must have Sailing Wind Wheel and 2x2 Micro

Method Manual to participate)

There are also bulk discounts for Sailing Schools and Yacht Clubs. Email: biz@sailingwindwheel.com for more information on ordering larger quantities for organizations.

Co-Author of *Marine Weather Log Book* with Lee Chesneau

This book will help boaters record and understand weather information pertinent to enjoying safe and pleasant sailing, whether for weekend trips, week-long excursions, or full ocean passages.

She is currently working on her next book *47 Things You Need to Remember When Docking a Boat.* Keeping with the theme of KISS - Keep It Simple Sweetheart, Captain Josie is simplifying all the things you need to remember when docking a boat. Most people only remember three things in their short term memory, which is why there is drama when learning to dock a boat. No matter how you cut it this is the toughest and most intimidating part of boating. But Captain Josie has watched hundreds of women blossom on a boat just by showing them that they can dock the boat.

Josie has also written two books, unrelated to sailing.

A.C.C.T.S. of Prayer in the Psalms,

The goal was to find out the true nature of God. She found all the verses in the Psalms, that describe God's true character. The acronym, ACTS follows the format of the Lord's prayer. A-Acknowledge, C-Confess, T-Thanksgiving, S-Suplication. The other C is Comfort. All the verses from the Psalms book are separated into these categories.

The second book, Chasing After God's Heart, is a supplement to the A.C.C.T.S. book. However, it can stand alone. All the words that describe God in the Psalms, are discussed in more detail and it is laid out like a workbook.

Visit the websites for purchasing all these books.
www.womensailing.com and www.sailingwindwheel.com

LaVergne, TN USA
18 January 2010
170265LV00004BA/3/P

ON WITH THE SHOW